Wild Plants I Have Known...
and Eaten

By Russ Cohen

With Illustrations by

Stephanie Letendre

WILD PLANTS I HAVE KNOWN AND EATEN

ISBN # 0-9719668-1-8
Price: $15.00

Photographs by Russ Cohen   2004 © Essex County Greenbelt Association, Inc.
Photographs by Elizabeth Darlington 2004 © Essex County Greenbelt Association, Inc.
Illustrations by Stephanie Letendre   2004 © Essex County Greenbelt Association, Inc.

Disclaimer: The information in this book is accurate to the best of the author's knowledge. Nevertheless, poisonous plants sometimes resemble edible ones, and they often grow side by side. Like some cultivated plants (rhubarb, potato, apple, etc.), some wild plants have both edible and poisonous parts. Some plants that may be edible when prepared correctly may be poisonous when prepared incorrectly. In addition, it is possible that a person could have an allergic or idiosyncratic adverse reaction to a plant whereas other people can consume it without ill effect. Therefore, the author, illustrator and publisher of this book assume no responsibility or liability for problems arising from the reader's misidentification, incorrect preparation, consumption or other use of wild plants. People who choose to eat wild plants do so at their own risk. Readers are urged to read carefully the safety precautions contained in the Introduction and in the specific plant descriptions. Readers are also encouraged to consult other wild plant field guides to assist in the accurate identification of any plant they intend to eat.

Published by: Essex County Greenbelt Association, Inc.
                  82 Eastern Avenue, Essex, MA 01929

                  Telephone: 978-768-7241
                  Fax: 978-768-3286
                  E-Mail: ecga@ecga.org
                  Website: www.ecga.org

Contact Russ Cohen at:
                  eatwild@rcn.com
                  Web page: http://users.rcn.com/eatwild/sched.htm

Photographs: Russ Cohen, Elizabeth Darlington
Editing: Jill Buchanan, zoomconsulting.net
Graphic Design: Jill Buchanan, zoomconsulting.net
Printing: Cricket Press

Printed on recycled paper
Sixth Printing 8/2014

Salt marshes at Greenbelt's Cox Reservation, Essex.

ABOUT THE PUBLISHER

For over five decades, the Essex County Greenbelt Association, a nonprofit land trust, has been conserving land of ecological, agricultural and scenic significance throughout Essex County, and has protected over 15,000 acres of land. By conserving the open space heritage of Essex County, we help ensure that future generations will continue to enjoy this key aspect of our quality of life.

We hope this book will inspire you to become more familiar with the edible bounty that surrounds us in our wild open spaces. We also hope that you will be encouraged and inspired to see what has been achieved over the last 50 years, and what is possible when members of the community work together with vision and dedication. To learn more about Greenbelt, please visit our website at www.ecga.org or call the office at 978-768-7241.

IN THE AUTHOR'S WORDS

I cannot say enough good things about what Greenbelt is doing to safeguard the essential nature of Essex County, striving to keep the region from being swallowed up in a sea of sterile subdivisions and strip malls. I hope any reader of this book that has not already done so will become a member of this highly worthwhile organization and/or the land trust(s) in your community. I have happily allowed Greenbelt to keep all of my share of the proceeds from the sale of this book. I am extremely grateful that, while remaining focused on and devoted to Greenbelt's primary mission of saving open space, Greenbelt's Executive Director Ed Becker endorsed the publication of this book. His decision reinforces the concept that, where compatible with other resource values, traditional uses of Essex County's rural landscape (like foraging) can play an important role in nourishing (literally as well as figuratively) people's connection to that landscape. Ed and Greenbelt are doing a tremendous service to foragers by explicitly allowing responsible foraging as a permitted activity on Greenbelt properties open to the public, and I hope many other land trusts and public land managers will follow their example.

ACKNOWLEDGEMENTS

I owe so much to so many people for helping to engender and nurture my fondness for edible wild plants. My parents, Lee and Rhoda Cohen, imbued me with a strong interest in and affection for the wooded landscape of my childhood home in Weston, Massachusetts. My dad is responsible for developing an ethic in me that open space should be accessible to people who act responsibly; and in fact, the trails on our family's land have always been open for people to enjoy respectfully. I owe much of my interest in and enjoyment of cooking to my mother's excellent example, learning from her how to prepare dishes by intuition as much as by following a recipe.

The person most responsible for providing the spark that ignited what has become for me a lifelong passion for eating wild plants is George Blakeslee, my high school biology teacher. More than two decades after finishing his mini-course on "Edible Botany," which was my first formal exposure to the subject, I tracked Mr. Blakeslee down and subsequently invited him to one of my wife Ellen and my Harvest Parties. It was a pleasure to share with him the more than three dozen dishes made with wild ingredients, so that he could see (and taste) firsthand what he helped to create.

I am thankful to others that helped fill in gaps in my knowledge of foraging and plant lore. Elizabeth (Libby) Darlington was one such person. Libby for many years taught edible wild plants classes for the New England Wild Flower Society (NEWFS) at the Rock Meadow Conservation Land in Belmont; I took over the classes when she retired in the 1990s, and later she kindly gave me her collection of foraging books and slide photographs, some of which are included in this book.

I am grateful to Pete Mirick, editor of Massachusetts Wildlife magazine for permitting me to borrow heavily from articles of mine they published in the 1990s, two of which served as a major source of raw material for this book. Dave Gabriel, whose graphics talent helps bring each issue of Massachusetts Wildlife magazine into being, was extremely helpful to me in getting several photographs into suitable shape for inclusion in this book.

I am extremely grateful that, while remaining focused on and devoted to its primary mission of saving open space, the Essex County Greenbelt Association agreed to publish this book. Jill Buchanan, Greenbelt's marketing consultant, came up with the original proposal to have Greenbelt publish some of my writing about foraging, and also edited and formatted this book with patience and skill.

Illustrator Stephanie Letendre created the many artistic yet accurate illustrations you see in this book. Toad Hall Bookstore in Rockport also deserves an honorable mention, as it provided Greenbelt with a small grant toward the cost of producing the book. I am much obliged to Sandy McDermott of Birchtree Studios for providing botanical drawings that informed many of the illustrations included in this book.

Last but not least, my ultimate and enduring gratitude goes to my wife Ellen Vliet Cohen, my chief companion for foraging (and just about everything else). In addition to being out in the field with me when she can, Ellen often cooks yummy dishes made with the stuff I've gathered on my own; in fact, several of the recipes in this book are primarily Ellen's work. Ellen showed tremendous patience and restraint during the time it took for this book to go from concept to reality. Now that the book is finally done, Ellen is looking forward to a break from the noise of my pounding out the text on the poor keyboard of our home computer.

I apologize in advance to any one whom I've inadvertently left out who may have played a role in bringing this book into being; whoever you are, thank you.

TABLE OF CONTENTS

Russ leads a group of enthusiasts in a wild edibles workshop

FOREWORD

A question I've often been asked over the 30+ years I've been gathering, eating, and teaching people about wild edibles is, "How did you get interested in this subject?"

I spent much of my free time as a child playing around the woods and streams near my home in Weston, Massachusetts, and thereby developed a strong fondness for nature. Other than the occasional family berry picking or nutting expedition, however, I had not much exposure to nor was I particularly interested in eating wild plants. I distinctly recall my father giving me one of Euell Gibbons' books (I think it was *Stalking the Wild Asparagus*) when I was in eighth grade, but I didn't even glance at it.

It wasn't until my sophomore year at Weston High School that I got fired up about foraging in a mini-course on Edible Botany, taught by Mr. Blakeslee. We learned about two dozen species of edible wild plants that grew around the high school grounds, and the course's finale was a "big feed," in which my classmates and I made and shared dishes from the plants we had learned about. The course got me so excited about foraging that I subsequently went to the town library and took out every book I could find on the topic. I taught myself over 50 more edible wild plant species in the following two years and, in my senior year of high school (1974), I taught a section of the Edible Botany class I had taken as a sophomore.

I continued to educate myself in and share my knowledge of edible wild plants throughout college and graduate school in upstate New York, Michigan and Ohio. Shortly after moving back to the Boston area in 1987, I resumed teaching about the edible wild plants of New England, starting with an Appalachian Mountain Club (AMC)-sponsored walk in my old stomping grounds in Weston. In all that time, however, I continued to steer away from foraging for wild mushrooms, as I was (along with most Americans) too afraid of making a fatal mistake.

Then, in the summer of 1989, I went on an AMC-sponsored conservation service trip to the Soviet Union, where we built hiking trails along the shores of Lake Baikal in Siberia. While there, I discovered that the Russians are passionate about wild mushrooms. On weekends, when many American families head to the mall, Russian families go mushroom hunting. I also noticed that even six-year-old kids were able to tell the difference between edible and poisonous species. At that point I said to myself, "If they can do it, I can do it," and subsequently lost my fear of mushrooms. I now enthusiastically forage for and teach people about edible wild mushrooms as well as plants.

I typically lead about two dozen edible wild plant (and mushroom) walks each year from May to October in the Boston area and elsewhere in New England. These walks range from two-hour evening urban walks to maritime expeditions along the coast to full-weekend forays in the mountains. An up-to-date schedule of the foraging walks and other programs I lead each year is posted on my web page (http://users.rcn.com/eatwild/sched. htm)

With increasing frequency over the last several years, I have been asked by my students, "So when's your book coming out?" I have focused most of my energy on teaching in the field instead of writing a book because I feel it addresses an important gap for many aspiring foragers who have trouble making the jump from reading about an edible wild plant to confidently finding, picking and eating that plant on their own. Discovering a plant with the help of an expert helps people overcome their fear of foraging by allowing them to see, feel, smell and (where appropriate) taste the actual plant or mushroom when they encounter it in the wild, something that they cannot do by reading a book or watching a video.

But if the truth be told, I have had a selfish motive for putting most of my energy into teaching classes rather than writing a book. I enjoy being present to see the looks of pleasure on people's faces and hear the exclamations of delight when I share my knowledge of and enthusiasm for foraging. I hope that by reading this book you will have a fine time looking for and eating some or all of the plants included here. I probably won't be with you to share that pleasant experience, but maybe some of you will write to tell me about your foraging adventures, so I can share in the fun you are having with this book.

Why did I choose to write my first book about edible wild plants in Essex County? I grew up and now live a short distance away from Essex County, and some of my favorite foraging spots are there. Of the 14 plant species featured in this book, I pick a lot of Hickory nuts, Autumn Olive and Barberries in Essex County. I also find and gather edible seaweeds, Beach Peas, Beach Plums, Day Lilies, Rose Hips, Wild Lettuce and many other species of edible wild plants and mushrooms in Essex County.

The main reason I picked Essex County as the area of focus for this book, however, is that the Essex County Greenbelt Association asked me to. Actually, Jill Buchanan, Greenbelt's development director at the time, asked me to write a chapter on edible wild plants for the *Greenbelt Guidebook*. When I submitted my first two plant writeups, she realized that my verbose writing style wouldn't lend itself well to the *Guidebook's* condensed format. She also realized that my writing would likely appeal to a larger audience. (All 41 plants covered in the book can readily be found elsewhere in southern New England, and many much further than that.) So

Greenbelt decided to put out this book as a stand-alone publication and make it available to the general public. I hope after reading it you agree that their decision was a good one.

My choice of the title for this book, *Wild Plants I Have Known... and Eaten,* was inspired by the title of another nature book written just over 100 years ago. *Wild Animals I Have Known*, written by Ernest Thompson Seton, was published by Scribners in 1898. Seton (who changed his name from Ernest Seton Thompson) was born in England but emigrated to Canada with his family at an early age. Seton became a passionate and detailed observer of wildlife and was appointed chief naturalist for the province of Manitoba in 1881. *Wild Animals I Have Known* is considered to be one of the earliest examples of nature writing based on scientific observation instead of romanticized (and often inaccurate) depictions of wild animal behavior. Seton later went on to co-found with Lord Baden-Powell the Boy Scouts in 1910, and wrote most of the original *Boy Scout Handbook.*

PART ONE
THE BASICS

Violets

WHETTING YOUR WILD APPETITE

How's this for a menu: Begin with a steaming bowl of Cream of Stinging Nettle Soup or Cattail Chowder, accompanied by crisp Groundnut Chips, moist Juneberry Muffins or fragrant Black Locust Fritters; follow with Jerusalem Artichokes *au Gratin*, Pokeweed Frittata or Milkweed Egg Puff; and top off with a slice of Strawberry-Knotweed Pie, Autumn Olive Fruit Leather or several Barberry-Hickory Nut Thumbprint Cookies. Wash it all down with a cold glass of Sumacade or a spicy mug of Sassafras Tea. If this bill of fare hasn't stimulated your appetite, I hope it has at least aroused your curiosity. In case you hadn't noticed, the factor these dishes share in common is that they are made primarily from wild ingredients.

While some may hold the notion that wild plants are repugnant to the palate and only worth resorting to in an emergency, many wild plants match or even exceed in flavor the best a supermarket has to offer. In addition, many edible wild plants contain considerably higher levels of vitamins and minerals than do their cultivated counterparts.

Why is it then that more people don't know about and partake of the over 150 species of edible wild plants growing in New England? The most obvious explanation is that in modern American society's high-tech rush toward affluence and convenience, we have left behind some of the simpler pleasures of earlier eras. Not so long ago (before the Second World War), most people utilized many edible wild plants, and perhaps spent pleasant Sunday afternoons nutting or berry-picking. Some industrious rural children earned pocket money through foraging, as the fruits of their labor occasionally made an appearance in the Boston produce markets.

Today's kids and their parents are more likely to spend Sunday afternoons at the mall or playing video games, and are thus becoming increasingly alienated from nature. There are, however, a few folks who choose to swim against this current and reconnect to the great outdoors through their taste buds. It is to current or potential members of this latter group that I offer a "taste" of the wild botanical delights waiting to be discovered.

I've chosen in this book to highlight 14 of my favorite edible wild plants as well as provide tasty tidbits about 27 more species. They are all fine flavored, relatively easy to find in Essex County and elsewhere and (with one small exception) difficult to confuse with any poisonous wild look-alikes. I encourage you to consult field guides to the flora of your region to help you positively identify any species you intend to eat (see the Bibliography on page 75 for suggestions).

Before getting into the delicious details of these 41 species, however, it's important to learn the basics of identifying, gathering and eating wild plants in an enjoyable, safe and environmentally responsible manner.

Why Forage?

Developing your foraging skills can enrich and enliven all the time you spend outdoors, whether it be in a park or vacant lot in downtown Boston, the beautiful rural countryside of Essex County, the seacoast, the mountains, the suburbs, just about anywhere.

As is true for birding, it is wise to obtain accurate guides to the flora of the particular place you are visiting. Unlike birding, however, foraging will not necessarily compel you to get up at the crack of dawn, nor will it give you a crick in your neck from staring up into the canopy.

Eating wild plants can be a potent means of expressing and nourishing your strong spiritual connection to nature. Speaking personally, I spent much of my childhood happily playing around by myself in the woods and streams near my home in Weston, Massachusetts. The woods became my welcoming sanctuary from the stresses of school where, not being an athlete nor a particularly good student, I felt I did not fit in. The woods also provided me with the solace and comfort I was unable to find in conventional religion. Nature itself became my "church," and it is there that I learned to celebrate communion. Instead of wine and wafers, however, I gathered and ate wild berries, roots, nuts and the like.

Foraging can also be a very sensual endeavor. You will experience the outdoors through your taste buds, eyes, and ears. Many wild plants and mushrooms have exotic flavors and/or textures that are difficult if not impossible to replicate in their cultivated counterparts.

Simply put, foraging is fun. The chance to be *al fresco* in natural surroundings and get a little exercise while helping yourself (in moderation) to nature's larder makes an outing all the more satisfying. You may also find some enjoyment in processing wild edibles once home, as the rhythm of shelling nuts and peeling stalks has a relaxing, almost meditative quality to it (like knitting). And, it is wonderfully rewarding to share with others what you have gathered and cooked into pies, preserves, casseroles and other delectable dishes.

Ostrich Fern fiddleheads

Foraging will also enable you to come up with a greater variety and complexity of dishes than if you relied on supermarket produce alone. Drying and/or freezing your raw materials and finished products will make your dishes interesting year-round. For example, my wife Ellen and I keep a freezer stocked with wild edibles including: steamed Stinging Nettle greens, several varieties of wild mushroom duxelles (a mixture of finely chopped mushrooms and onions, slowly cooked in butter until it forms a thick paste); White Oak Acorn flour; Cattail pollen; shelled Hickory Nuts and Black Walnuts, along with cookies and other desserts made from them; frozen raw Sulphur Shelf and Hen-of-the-Woods mushrooms;

frozen raw Black Locust Flowers; blanched and frozen Ostrich Fern Fiddleheads, Milkweed buds and pods and Pokeweed shoots, along with a frozen raw Strawberry-Knotweed and several wild fruit pies. Our pantry is filled a variety of wild jams and jellies, dried mushrooms, herbs, flowers, seaweed, dried and stewed fruit, and syrups as well as a large supply of Autumn Olive Fruit Leather (see Chapter Twelve).

Foraging will greatly sharpen your observation skills as you begin to take note of factors that influence when and where the wild edibles can be found. You will learn to keep closer track of the seasons of the year, weather forecasts and patterns, and plants that share similar habitats. After a while, you may develop a sort of "sixth sense" for foraging. One day, while walking a trail, you will pick up clues that an edible plant you are looking for is likely to be nearby. You'll go around a bend in the trail and, sure enough, there it is. Or, you will amaze friends and family members by being able to spot an edible wild plant or mushroom while speeding by at 55 mph.

Finally, it is reassuring to know that if done properly, foraging has negligible adverse impacts on wild plants, wild mushrooms and their habitats. The growing concern over the harm caused by humans to the natural world has led some people and environmental organizations to adopt what I call the "Velvet Rope" approach to the outdoors — as if nature was bordered by the maroon-colored ropy railings you see at art museums. You can lean over the rope to look, but you can't actually touch or interact with anything (never mind picking and eating it). Although the underlying motives behind the "Velvet Rope" approach and similar programs (such as "Leave No Trace") are certainly laudable, their strictures may unduly discourage people from foraging. This is also a tragedy. It is important to take time to enjoy and celebrate the wondrous bounty of nature. Few other pursuits make one as highly aware of humanity's dependence upon nature for our continued physical and spiritual well-being.

I do not mean by these remarks to find fault with those people or organizations that seek to impose a "no touch" policy on specific, ecologically significant habitats of a highly threatened and/or sensitive nature. I merely feel that we have more to gain from encouraging (or at least tolerating) environmentally responsible foraging in appropriate locations than by enforcing an unduly rigid barrier between us and the natural world.

WHERE TO FORAGE

Though this book doesn't suggest specific properties, various habitats in Essex County make for good foraging. In general, places with good sun exposure are prime locations for foraging. Some of these include "shaggy" spots such as old fields and meadows that haven't been mowed recently, or "edges," be they along soccer fields, water bodies, pathways, lightly-traveled roads and railroads and power lines.

Organic farms are some of the best places to gather wild edible plants (not the cultivated crops, but the weeds and other wild plants growing in and adjacent to organic farm fields). There are several reasons why organic farms make great foraging locations: first, organic farmers never use chemical pesticides or fertilizers so you don't have to worry about artificial toxins on or in any of the plants you pick; second, organic farmers periodically remove weeds by hand and/or mechanically, so if your timing is right you can gather enough of the edible weeds to feed an army; third, many weeds, such as Chickweed (*Stellaria media*) and Purslane (*Portulaca oleracea*) prefer the same type of rich, organic soil as cultivated crops, so you can often find larger and tastier versions of these at organic farms. Edible wild root crops like Wild Carrot (*Daucus carota*) and Evening Primrose (*Oenothera biennis*), which tend to produce scrawny roots in poor soil, can produce roots as big as domesticated carrots at organic farms. Furthermore, the same trace elements, minerals and other healthful goodies present in the living, organic soil that help make cultivated organic vegetables so nutritious are getting into the wild edibles growing there as well. Last but not least, organic farm fields are typically bordered by woodlots, and between the two you can often find some great edge habitat for wild fruit trees, nut trees and berry bushes.

Essex County stretches from Salisbury to Methuen to Saugus to Rockport.

If you don't know of any organic farms in your area, the Northeast Organic Farming Association (NOFA) (www.nofamass.org, (978) 355-2853 in Massachusetts) maintains a list. Once you find one, get permission to forage from the farm manager. Managers of organic farms (indeed, farmers in general) are usually quite amenable to gathering wild edibles on their property. It is worth developing a friendly relationship with your local organic farmer(s) as they are often eager to learn about the culinary qualities of weeds and may even try some themselves. (It probably wouldn't hurt to buy some cultivated crops from their farmstand when you are finished gathering your wild edibles.)

Another great place to forage in Essex County is along its extensive coastal shoreline, which provides habitat for dozens of edible wild plant species. At least six species of edible seaweeds can be found within the intertidal zone, for example. Some, like Irish Moss (*Chrondrus crispus*) and Dulse (*Rhodymenia palmata*), like to grow at or below the low-tide mark, often on or around surf-pounded rocky shorelines. If you are too squeamish to gather there, wait for a storm to tear the plants loose and wash them up on a nearby beach.

Dulse seaweed (Rhodymenia

Another spot to look for wild edibles in the region is at the landward edges of beaches and salt marshes, the preferred habitat of such salt-tolerant species as Sea Rocket (*Cakile edentula*), Orach (*Atriplex spp.*); Beach Pea (*Lathyrus maritimus*), Glasswort (*Salicornia spp.*), and Silverweed (*Potentilla anserina*). On the backside of the dunes, away from the salt water, but still occasionally reached by salt spray and strong coastal winds, you can find such coastal species as Beach Plum (*Prunus maritima*), Salt Spray Rose (*Rosa rugosa*) and Bayberry (*Myrica pensylvanica*). In addition to taking special care not to pick one of the rare coastal species (see Part Two), avoid picking from busy harbors and other heavily-used shoreline areas as well as from properties where foraging is prohibited.

Whether or not you can gather wild edibles from privately- or publicly-owned conservation land depends upon who owns the property and the conservation purposes sought to be advanced. Properties owned by the Massachusetts Audubon Society (the Ipswich River Wildlife Sanctuary in Topsfield, for example) are managed as ecological refuges for all forms of flora and fauna, so collecting of any kind is expressly prohibited. Some conservation lands (such as some Greenbelt properties) allow more active use of the land. Gathering wild edibles is allowed on the Greenbelt properties listed in the *Greenbelt Guidebook* (for more information on how to obtain a *Guidebook*, go to www.ecga.org), although it is assumed that all foragers know and follow good conservation practices, including taking special care not to deplete the less common edible species.

If you don't know whether foraging on a particular property is permitted, ask the land owner or land manager. Regulations governing the use of wildlife management areas (WMAs) maintained by the Massachusetts Division of Fisheries and Wildlife expressly allow people to pick berries and other fruits, nuts and mushrooms without a permit as long as it is for personal consumption [see 321 CMR 3.01(1)(f)]. (Essex County has quite a lot of acreage in WMAs; go to http://www.mass.gov/eea/agencies/dfg/dfw/maps-destinations/wildlife-management-areas.html for more information.) Such "benign" types of foraging (see "Conservation Ethics," page 14) may also be condoned on public parklands, although individual park rangers and managers may vary in their level of personal comfort with it. It is a control issue as much as a conservation one; most park managers/rangers simply like to keep tabs on what's going on in their park. Nevertheless, it is courteous to ask the park manager first before picking. (It's a nice touch if you offer them some of what you pick.)

More intrusive forms of foraging, such as stripping the flowers or foliage off of plants or pulling up whole plants by the roots, are generally not allowed on public parklands. Even so, managers may be willing to relax the rules a bit depending upon what and where you want to harvest. For example, if you ask a park manager permission to dig up Burdock (*Arctium spp.*) roots growing alongside his parking lot, he'll probably hand you a shovel.

The last bit of foraging etiquette you should consider is the aesthetic value of many edible wild plants. Many people walk in the woods and fields just for the sheer pleasure of seeing nature's beauty. If you are interested in gathering plants or plant parts with aesthetic value, like wildflowers, try to find an out-of-the-way harvesting location (e.g., away from popular walking paths) where it is unlikely that your picking will degrade others' visual experience.

WHEN TO FORAGE

Once you have familiarized yourself with the details of how to identify plants you can use the spreadsheets in the Appendix as guides for when to forage for particular species. The "***When to Pick Edible Wild Plants in New England***" sheets in the Appendix reflect my observations over seven years of when edible wild berries, nuts, roots, etc. were ripe and/or available for harvesting in the Boston area.

The same information is presented in two formats: alphabetically (by common name) and chronologically. On the alphabetical list, simply look down the list of names until the desired plant is found, and then look across that particular line; the darkened boxes represent the week(s) that plant part is available for harvesting in the Boston area. For example, for Stinging Nettle greens, look down the alphabetical list for "Stinging Nettle," and then across that line to see that Stinging Nettle greens are prime for harvesting for four weeks (April 1-30) in the Boston area. On the chronological list, simply start at the top of the spreadsheet to locate the current date, and then move down the appropriate column(s) to the darkened boxes to find out which plant parts are available at that time. For example, let's say it's the Fourth of July and you want to do a little foraging; find the July 1-8 column at the top of the spreadsheet and look down the column to find that Beach Peas, Black Raspberries, Day Lily flowers and flower buds and Juneberries are all typically available for picking on that date in the Boston area.

Note, however, that some wild plants (Japanese Knotweed, Jerusalem Artichokes, Juneberries, Stinging Nettles and Pokeweed, for example) are larger and/or more distinctive-looking and easier to find at times of the year that differ from the best times to harvest as stated on the "When to Pick..." spreadsheets. Skilled foragers develop the ability to recognize and locate edible wild plants when they are out of season, memorize (or write down) those locations, and then go back to visit those spots at the appropriate harvesting time.

The information in these spreadsheets should save you considerable time and guesswork in gathering wild edibles in prime comestible condition. Perhaps they will inspire you to record your own observations and compile them into a similar spreadsheet for your favorite foraging locations.

PART TWO
MORE USEFUL INFORMATION

Beach Pea

This section of the book provides more information about how to forage safely and responsibly, but first I would like to share with you my view on two types of foraging which I personally don't engage in but which my students have expressed curiosity about over the years: harvesting edible wild plants for money or for survival.

Wild foods commercialism

Wild edibles (especially wild mushrooms) are popping up with increasing frequency on the menus of upscale restaurants and grocery shelves, due in large part to our increasing affluence and sophistication of our collective palates. However, there are several reasons why the commercialization of edible wild plants has not occurred on a large scale (at least not yet in New England).

Pickled Ox-eye Daisy flower buds.

First, many wild plants are ephemeral in nature; they need to be eaten soon after gathering, or they lose much of their appeal. In contrast, most produce items in supermarkets have been engineered to sit around for days in a vegetable bin.

Second, the availability of many wild crops is very seasonally dependent and unpredictable. Their abundance can vary considerably from year to year depending upon the weather, how much that location has been harvested from, ecological succession and changes in land use. Most foragers can find what they need for themselves and their families, but it is unlikely to be enough to interest a supermarket chain. Produce retailers and most restaurants count on their suppliers to furnish a predictable quantity of product on a regular basis.

In spite of these obstacles, some edible wild plant species are gathered from the wild and then sold to restaurants and/or grocery stores. Fiddleheads (the young unfurled fronds of the Ostrich Fern, *Matteucia struthiopteris*) are probably the best-known example of this in New England. For some people, especially those that live in rural areas with relatively few employment opportunities, gathering and selling wild plants like fiddleheads can be a significant source of much-needed extra income. That said, going beyond foraging for personal use to gathering wild plants for commercial purposes (often referred to as wildcrafting) can change one's relationship with the plants. Money is a powerful motivating factor, and many (although certainly not all) commercial pickers may be unable to resist the temptation to harvest more than is ecologically sustainable. Such overharvesting could eventually extirpate (i.e., make locally extinct) wild edibles in some locales. Though this is not yet a problem for any edible wild plants in New England, it is for some medicinal plants. Herbs such as Ginseng (*Panax quinquefolius*) and Goldenseal (*Hydrastis canadensis*) have been overcollected by people seeking to sell them to the herbal medicinal trade.

In addition, consumers of commercially-gathered wild edibles who confine their relationships with wild edibles solely to that of a passive diner or purchaser are missing much of the essence of foraging: the direct connection between themselves and the places where the wild edibles are found.

Going into the woods and fields to find and gather up wild foods oneself is, in my opinion, the best way to get the greatest all-round benefit from wild foods. In addition to experiencing all the wonderful and exotic flavors and textures wild foods can offer, locating, harvesting and preparing these wild foods themselves enables foragers to experience the atavistic thrill of reconnecting with our roots as a species. After all, for the vast majority of Homo sapiens' time on the Earth we were a hunting and gathering species. It has only been relatively recently that our society has lost contact with that fundamental element of our nature. The act of foraging can satisfy our deep-seated, primeval hunter-gatherer instincts in a way that is simply unobtainable through a restaurant or supermarket produce section.

Nevertheless, perhaps some folks unfamiliar with foraging will enjoy the taste of wild plants served to them at a restaurant and their interest will be sufficiently piqued to try gathering and preparing wild food on their own. If so, then the restaurant will have helped reconnect folks with nature after all.

Before leaving this topic, it is worth noting the burgeoning "slow food" movement, begun in 1986 by Italian food writer and activist Carlo Petrini. Petrini recognized that the industrialization of food and the proliferation of fast food franchises across the globe are standardizing taste and leading to the annihilation of thousands of local food varieties and flavors. Slow Food, the organization created by Petrini that year, now has a worldwide membership and its American affiliate (Slow Food USA, www.slowfoodusa.org) is organized into local chapters of like-minded aficionados (there is one in the Boston area). The organization purports that pleasure and quality in everyday life can be achieved by slowing down, respecting the convivial traditions of the table and celebrating the diversity of the earth's bounty.

Although the Slow Food movement's objectives of supporting local farms and artisanal food makers are laudable, I cannot help but observe that the main focus of Slow Food aficionados is on purchasing food grown, harvested and/or prepared by others rather than doing it themselves. By continuing to allow a financial transaction to intrude between themselves and the food, I believe they miss out on the ultimate and complete "slow food" experience of actively engaging in harvesting, preparing and eating their own food, whether by raising it at home or hunting or gathering it from the wild.

Wild Edibles for Survival?

Some folks are motivated to learn about edible wild plants because they want to be prepared in case our conventional food supply is destroyed in a terrorist attack, war or other civil breakdown. It is certainly understandable in the post-9/11 climate that some people would fear future attacks and want to be prepared accordingly. Yet, one is better off laying up a reserve supply of conventional foodstuffs and water than expecting to survive primarily on food gathered from the wild. Also, while wild food is relatively plentiful during the growing season, knowledge of wild foods is of limited value when the ground is frozen. That being said, if, God forbid, some sort of long-term natural or human-caused disruption of our food supply should occur, knowing which wild plants are edible could certainly come in handy.

Others take a sort of "macho" approach to foraging, wanting to see how long they could survive in nature. There are two potential major downsides to this approach. First, with hunger as a powerful motivator, there's a good chance one will give in to the temptation to pick more than is ecologically sustainable; second, it is possible that starvation-induced delirium could cloud one's judgment and result in picking and eating poisonous plants or not preparing edible plants properly (e.g., failing to boil a plant first when necessary to remove toxins).

It is better to bring along an ample supply of food with you on trips into the outdoors, since wild crops tend to be very unpredictable. For example, when my wife Ellen and I go on a camping trip, we typically bring all the food we need for the trip. Yet, we often bring home as much as half of that food as we will have foraged for half of what we ate.

It is unlikely, however, that in this region you would ever find yourself in a life-threatening situation from lack of food. In Essex County and most of southern New England, you will likely be able to hike to the nearest convenience store long before you find yourself in serious danger of starving to death.

IS IT SAFE TO EAT WILD FOODS?

With very few exceptions, most poisonous wild plants found in New England taste bad, so it is strongly suggested to refrain from eating plants that taste bad. This does not mean that every edible wild plant is delicious in its raw state; many plants need to be cooked before they taste good. It does mean, however, that if you prepare an edible wild plant properly, the finished product should taste good.

Note, however, that this "bad taste" rule does not apply to wild mushrooms. Many of the most lethal mushroom varieties have an agreeable flavor. Like wild plants, the best way to learn wild mushrooms is with the help of other people, in the wild. We are very fortunate in the Boston area to have the Boston Mycological Club (BMC), an organization devoted in large part to helping people identify mushrooms in the wild. The BMC sponsors free mushroom "forays" at

Russ, pictured with King Bolete (Boletus edulis).

various outdoor locations throughout the Greater Boston area almost every Sunday during mushroom season. You can find more information on the BMC web site at www.bostonmycologicalclub.org. The North American Mycological Association (NAMA, www.namyco.org/clubs/index.html) has information on mushroom clubs outside the Greater Boston area. You can also read my article about edible/poisonous wild mushrooms, entitled, "Stalking the Wild Bolete and other Fungal Delights," which appeared in the Summer 1994 issue of <u>Massachusetts Wildlife</u> magazine. This article is posted on the web at http://users.rcn.com/eatwild/mushroom.htm. In addition, see the Bibliography for recommended books on mushroom foraging.

For plants, however, you can consider your taste buds as a back-up identification tool while foraging in New England. If you identify a plant you believe to be edible, it's okay to place a small morsel in your mouth momentarily, then spit it out. The worst that could happen is that you might feel a little queasy for a while (which might be psychological). If, however, you have cooked the plant according to instructions and it still tastes horrible, don't override the danger signal your taste buds are giving you; you may have made a mistake in identification.

Two apparent exceptions to the "poisonous plants taste bad" rule are Poison Hemlock (*Conium maculatum*) and Water Hemlock (*Cicuta maculata*), both very poisonous members of the Carrot or Parsley Family (Apiaceae, formerly known as the Umbelliferae for the Family's umbrella-like flower clusters) and not related to the Hemlock Tree (*Tsuga canadensis*). Socrates was made to drink a Poison Hemlock tea and subsequently died from it. A few years ago, two brothers from Wayland, Massachusetts, ate a root they believed to be Ginseng but turned out to be Poison or Water Hemlock. One of them died and the other became seriously ill.

Poison Hemlock

This was a tragic case of uninformed foraging. Although their roots bear superficial resemblance to each other, Ginseng and Poison Hemlock differ greatly in above-ground appearance and habitat. Ginseng (*Panax quinquefolius*), now an overcollected and all-too-uncommon medicinal (not culinary) plant, grows in deep, rich woods, has palmate, hickory-like leaves, red berries and rarely grows more than two feet high. In contrast, Poison Hemlock typically grows in open meadows along streams and ranges from 3-5 feet in height, with feathery carrot-like leaves. A careful forager would never confuse the two. That said, several edible wild members of the Apiaceae, including Wild Carrot (*Daucus carota*), Wild Parsnip (*Pastinaca sativa*) and Caraway (*Carum carvi*) closely resemble (as well as are closely related to) Poison or Water Hemlock, so foragers are strongly advised to take special care when contemplating eating any wild members of this botanical family.

Edible wild plants can be arranged on a line, with the easy-to-recognize plants at one end and the hard-to-identify plants with highly poisonous look-alikes at the other end. Many of the easy-to-recognize edible wild plants (such as Dandelion) are ones you probably already know. Stay at this safe end until you gain the necessary skills and confidence to explore plants at the more adventurous end.

I have noticed that folks interested in nature tend to fall into two camps: "lumpers" and "splitters." Birders tend to be splitters: they like to know the exact species or subspecies of each bird they observe, and part of the fun of birding is to engage in petty arguments with other birders about exactly what bird it was you all just spotted. On the other hand, foragers tend to be "lumpers." We basically want to know one thing: can we eat it or not? If the answer is yes, we tend not to be that concerned about the exact species or subspecies of what we choose to pick and eat.

One of the best ways to sharpen your botanical observation skills is to learn about plant families. Plants are grouped into botanical families by similarities in flower structure. Sometimes, just knowing what family a plant is in will tell you whether it is edible. For example, all wild members of the Mustard Family (Brassicaceae, formerly known as Cruciferae) and Mint Family (Lamiaceae, formerly known as Labiatae) that grow in New England are edible, but not all equally yummy. Whether or not and how you eat them depends on the flavor of the particular Mint or Mustard you have found. However, each family contains at least several members that are considered rare and protected in New England, so avoid picking the rare Mints and Mustards by confining your foraging for them to disturbed habitats like farm fields and streams.

Then there are the botanical families that have both fine, upstanding edible species and poisonous black sheep. Take the Nightshade Family, (the Solanaceae), for instance. Edible members include tomatoes, potatoes, eggplants and peppers, poisonous members include Jimson Weed, Belladonna, Deadly Nightshade and Tobacco. Other botanical families notorious for having many poisonous as well as edible relatives include the aforementioned Carrot or Parsley Family (Apiaceae) featuring the notorious Poison and Water Hemlocks, the Pea Family (Fabaceae, formerly known as the Leguminosae), the Heath Family (Ericaceae) and the Cashew Family (Anacardiaceae). Some beginning foragers simply choose not to pick anything from these latter families (especially the Carrot/Parsley Family) just to make certain they don't pick a poisonous family member by mistake.

Every so often, after I point out a poisonous plant or mushroom on one of my walks, someone will ask, "Just how poisonous is that?" I usually respond with a joke along the lines of, "Are you really asking, 'How much would I need if I wanted to take care of someone I didn't like?'" Seriously, the answer depends as much or more on the the individual eating the toxin as the poison itself. Kids, the elderly, and people with depressed immune systems or otherwise in frail health are at greater risk of getting seriously poisoned. In most cases, however, the poisoned individual will vomit up and/or excrete the poisonous compound(s) before they do any long-term damage.

It is possible that you or others may be allergic to one or more edible wild plants or mushrooms and not know it simply because you had never been exposed to that particular food before. Thus you may want to follow the standard advice of eating a modest amount of any wild food you are eating for the first time just to see if you experience any adverse reactions to it. If you are generally not allergic to cultivated plants and/or mushrooms, it is highly unlikely that you will be allergic to their wild counterparts, as chemically they are very similar to each other. That said, if you are allergic to a particular cultivated plant, then it is certainly possible you could be allergic to its wild cousins as well.

OTHER SAFETY ISSUES

The hazards one is exposed to while foraging may actually pose a greater health risk than the plants themselves. These hazards can be natural, man-made or both.

For example, pesticide residues, contaminated soil or other harmful pollutants can get into the wild plants you pick and eat. However, through judicious selection of harvesting locations and other common sense precautions, one can minimize (but unfortunately not eliminate) exposure to these and other environmental health hazards. Avoid any heavily manicured landscapes like closely-cropped lawns, shrubbery and golf courses, as there is a good possibility the foliage has been doused with insecticides, herbicides, fungicides and other chemicals. Also, avoid areas you suspect to be contaminated, such as current or former industrial sites and water bodies receiving significant discharges from sewage treatment plants or runoff from city streets, livestock pens and the like. The margins of heavily-traveled roadsides fall into this category, as they tend to accumulate exhaust fumes and other automobile-related pollutants. Also, try to avoid picking within areas of urban or suburban parks subject to heavy human and/or dog activity.

Refrain from picking plants with spotted or wilted leaves or other signs of stress, as this may indicate that they have been exposed to toxins. Urban and roadside soils can accumulate lead and other heavy metals.

Some plants take toxins up into their tissues, others don't. In general, the highest concentrations of heavy metals and other pollutants are found in a plant's leaves, followed by its roots, with the lowest levels in its fruit. Even if you do ingest some toxins, unless wild edibles collected from contaminated areas become a staple of your diet, your level of exposure is relatively low.

Then there are the health threats posed by ticks, bees, mosquitoes and other insects, as well as the disease-causing microbes they may carry or that may be encountered elsewhere in the environment. Microbial hazards include the Lyme Disease bacterium, West Nile virus and Giardia protozoan, as well as a host of lesser-known but equally dangerous pathogens. Most of these biological hazards potentially affect anyone that spends time outdoors, but probably foragers even more so, as we are prone to wander off-trail and push through the undergrowth in search of a tasty meal. Here, the best wisdom is to follow the standard precautions applicable to anyone spending time outside. For example, you can prevent bug bites by covering your skin; avoid water-borne diseases by not drinking directly from streams; wash and/or cook wild edibles before eating them, particularly those that may have been exposed to animal feces or other pathogens. The Center for Disease Control and Prevention (CDC)'s website, www.cdc.gov, is a good place to go for accurate information on prevention of and/or treatment for Lyme Disease, Giardia and other pathogens.

This frank discussion of health risks can be a bit unsettling, even for people who have been foraging for decades. In addition, faithfully following these preventative measures in all situations requires a level of discipline beyond the reach of many (especially when berry picking). It comes down to the degree of risk one is willing to take. Once you determine your personal risk/comfort level, you can decide when and how you want to forage (or not) and do so accordingly.

13

Foraging by and/or with children

Children's smaller bodies are more susceptible than adults' to being adversely affected by eating poisonous plants or mushrooms, so one needs to use particular care when foraging and eating wild foods with children. That said, foraging is a wonderful way for children to build a loving relationship and lifelong fascination with the natural world. Once they know what to look for, kids often make highly skilled foragers (it may help that they are closer to the ground). I have also heard from parents of ordinarily finicky eaters that their children will consume with great relish any wild food they were involved in picking and/or preparing.

It wasn't that long ago that kids spent most of their free time unsupervised, playing outdoors, looking for and eating wild nuts, berries and other wild edibles. In fact, many of the older foraging books begin describing a wild plant with the phrase, "Every boy is familiar with eating this plant." Nowadays, most kids would be hard-pressed to identify many wild plants at all, never mind wild edibles. It has not helped that the continuing conversion of open space to development has put nature (and foraging opportunities) increasingly out of reach of many youngsters.

Foraging is a fun activity that can help "turn up the volume" on walks, hikes, and other outdoor excursions, thereby successfully competing against shopping and web surfing for kids' limited attention spans.

How young is too young to get kids involved in foraging? It depends somewhat on the individual child. Some eight-year-olds know more about edible wild plants or mushrooms than most adults. It also depends on how thoroughly versed you are as parents, teachers, or scoutmasters about wild edibles. It isn't necessary to have a Ph.D in botany to teach foraging; just stick to the species you know well. Likewise, until you are sure your kids know what they are doing and are fully cognizant of the risks involved, carefully instruct them to bring whatever it is they would like to eat to you first and get your go-ahead before they chow down.

Ellen Vliet Cohen with Indian Cucumber (Medeola virginiana).

Conservation ethics

Wherever you go to forage for wild plants, it is very important to practice good conservation ethics. In addition to being considerate of a plant species' potential rarity and/or value to wildlife, it is important to make sure you are picking from a good-sized patch of plants, and make sure that you leave more than enough to ensure the plant's continued survival. If the patch is too small to harvest without potentially threatening its sustainability at that location, simply keep looking until you find a larger one. Native Americans had a ritualistic way of following this advice. Rather than harvesting the first patch they encountered, they placed an offering of tobacco or some other valuable token there and continued to hunt until they found another patch.

Using the "***Checklist and Rarity Ranking***" sheet (see Appendix) will help ensure plants' sustainability. The Checklist and Rarity Ranking sheet contains (in alphabetical order by common name) most of the edible wild plants found in New England. Consider it as a sort of edible wild plant "life list," similar to those used by serious birders to record bird species they have seen during their lifetimes. Foragers can use the checklist to keep track of edible wild plants they have identified and/or eaten.

Each plant is assigned a grade ranging from A+ to C-. The "higher" the grade, the less you have to worry about any adverse ecological consequences of harvesting. Species in the "A" category tend to be so abundant and/or invasive that there is no need for restraint; plants in the "C" category tend to be uncommon and/or ecologically sensitive species which, while they may still be harvested in modest amounts, should be harvested judiciously. You will find a detailed explanation of each letter grade on the reverse side of the sheet.

Your influence on a plant's ability to survive largely depends on the part(s) of the plant you pick. For example, berry picking and nut gathering (as well as mushroom hunting) are generally considered to be relatively benign forms of foraging because these fruiting bodies merely serve as an organism's seed or spore dispersal device. Plants and mushrooms typically lose many of these fruiting bodies in reproduction. Indeed, many plants evolved to produce large quantities of fleshy, good-tasting fruits and nuts so that animals would eat them and then disperse at least some of the seeds to new growing locations. As long as you leave the main body of the organism intact (e.g., you do not pull off whole branches of trees while gathering fruits or nuts), that plant's ability to produce a good crop of fruit or nuts the following season should not be adversely affected.

You must be more circumspect when conducting more intrusive foraging methods, such as gathering entire plants, stripping off their foliage and/or digging them up to harvest the roots. Doing so could kill the plants and potentially extirpate that species. It is particularly important to use caution with "B" or "C" species in the Rarity Ranking list. It is usually okay to pull or dig up a few plants of "B" or "C"-ranked species, provided you have found a particularly large patch of them. You should nevertheless take care not to dig up more than one of every dozen or so of these plants in one spot. There is, however, little need to worry when pulling up weeds, invasives and other "A"-ranked plants. Furthermore, some plant species, such as Day Lilies (*Hemerocallis spp.*) and Jerusalem Artichokes (*Helianthus tuberosus*) (see Chapter Thirteen), often grow in patches too thickly for their own good and can benefit from thinning out some of their tubers.

ENDANGERED AND INVASIVE PLANTS

An important conservation question foragers should ask themselves is, 'Could I mistakenly pick a plant on the state's list of rare and endangered species?' You can find the Massachusetts List of Endangered, Threatened and Special Concern Species (a.k.a. the "T and E" list) either by requesting a copy from the Massachusetts Division of Fisheries and Wildlife's Natural Heritage and Endangered Species Program (NHESP) by calling (508) 389-6360 or by viewing it online at http://www.mass.gov/eea/agencies/dfg/dfw/natural-heritage/species-information-and-conservation/rare-plants/. Relatively few of the plant species on the state's "T and E" list are edible, and since the state's rare plant species tend to be confined to pristine and/or unusual habitats, you are unlikely to encounter them outside of those locations. In general, if you see a plant growing in an unusual or pristine habitat that looks similar to but not exactly the same as a common edible wild plant, you should refrain from picking it to make sure you don't pick a rare cousin by mistake.

Each state's Natural Heritage Program maintains its own "T and E" list, and readers are advised to familiarize themselves with the "T and E" plants in the state(s) where they forage to avoid harvesting species considered rare in that location.

Essex County's largest area of unusual habitat is its extensive coastal shoreline. It is possible while foraging along the shore to come across such state- or federally-listed rare plants as Seabeach Amaranth (*Amaranthus pumilus*) and Seabeach Dock (*Rumex pallidus*), two very rare coastal cousins of the common farm, garden and/or roadside weeds, Amaranth (*Amaranthus retroflexus*) and Curled Dock (*Rumex crispus*).

So, if you are interested in harvesting Amaranth or Curled Dock, simply confine your foraging to inland habitats. This advice is not intended to discourage you from foraging along the coastline, as it is one of the best places in Essex County to hunt for wild edibles. It merely requires a higher level of diligence to ensure that rare plants aren't picked by mistake.

In fact, it is much more likely that a wild plant you are interested in picking and eating is on another state list of a much more sinister nature: the list of 66 plant species deemed to be invasive by the Massachusetts Invasive Plant Advisory Group (MIPAG, http://www.massnrc.org/MIPAG). The NHESP's "Invasive Plant Information" web page (http://www.mass.gov/eea/agencies/dfg/dfw/natural-heritage/land-protection-and-management/invasive-species/invasive-plants.html) provides more background information on this issue. *A Guide to Invasive Plants In Massachusetts*, a useful printed 79-page booklet produced by the NHESP in collaboration with several partners, providing color photos and other descriptive characteristics of the 66 species, is available from the NHESP at (508) 389-6360 or at the New England Wild Flower Society (NEWFS, www.newfs.org, (508)877-7630.) A regional invasives database is maintained at the Invasive Plant Atlas of New England (IPANE) website, http://www.eddmaps.org/ipane/.

Garlic Mustard (Alliaria petiolata)

Ecologists tend to despise the invasive species on these botanical blacklists because the plants usurp habitat from native species. Nevertheless, at least two dozen invasive and/or otherwise weedy species found in this region are edible, including Common Mallow (*Malva neglecta*), Garlic Mustard (*Alliaria petiolata*), Dame's Rocket (*Hesperus matronalis*), Pineapple Weed (*Matricaria matricarioides*), Purslane (*Portulaca oleracea*) and Sow Thistle (*Sonchus oleraceus*) (*oleracea/us*, roughly translated from Latin, means "good enough to be a garden vegetable").

Of the species featured in this book, Autumn Olive (*Elaeagnus umbellata*) and Japanese Knotweed (*Fallopia japonica,* formerly known as *Polygonum cuspidatum)* have the dubious honor of appearing at or near the top of the MIPAG blacklist, while Black Locust (*Robinia pseudoacacia*) and European Barberry (*Berberis vulgaris*) are given a dishonorable mention. Most ecologists would be thrilled, however, if you picked and ate as many of these invasive plants as you possibly could (provided you didn't help spread them around in the process).

WILDLIFE FOOD SUPPLIES

Many erstwhile foragers are afraid that harvesting wild edibles may deprive wildlife of needed sustenance. If you make sure there is plenty of what you want before you start picking and plenty left over when you are done, then you are more than likely leaving enough food for the wild animals. You can take additional solace in knowing that not all the plants people eat are ones that wild animals eat because our digestive systems and taste buds differ. Much of the most important food for wildlife either doesn't taste good or is harmful for humans to eat. Poison Ivy buds and berries, for example, are some of the most important sources of winter food for many bird and mammal species.

Nevertheless, if you wish to be extra conscientious on this matter, you may want to read the book, *American Wildlife and Plants: A Guide to Wildlife Food Habits* by A.C. Martin, H.S. Zim and A.L. Nelson (published by Dover Press and available through the Massachusetts Association of Conservation Commissions (617) 489-3930), which will help you identify plants that are important to wildlife in your area.

On a related topic: you may see a mushroom with an animal bite taken out of it and wonder if you can eat it. The answer is "No" (or at least "not necessarily") for two reasons: first, because, as mentioned above, there isn't 100% overlap between what people can eat and what animals eat; and second, because you don't know what happened to that animal after it ate that mushroom. It might have died a horrible death. Animals can make mistakes too, so don't rely on them.

A FINAL WORD OF ADVICE

I hope the foregoing introduction has whetted your appetite to pick and eat wild edibles. I also hope it has given you a realistic picture of the various health risks posed by eating wild plants and by foraging in general. My final word of advice: don't eat anything you are not comfortable with eating, whether you are concerned about having picked the wrong plant, that the area that you harvested from is contaminated, or any other reason.

It is finally time to unveil the secrets of the wild ingredients making up the proposed menu described at the beginning of this book. The following 14 chapters are arranged in rough chronological order according to when the edible portion(s) of that particular plant are available for harvesting, beginning in the spring and continuing on until the following winter.

PART THREE

PLANT PROFILES

AND RECIPES

Wild Grapes

CHAPTER ONE

STINGING NETTLE: BAD FOR YOUR OUTSIDE, GOOD FOR YOUR INSIDE

Stinging Nettle (*Urtica dioica*) was introduced (probably unintentionally) to North America many years ago from Europe, where it is well-known and appreciated by many. Despite its unappetizing name, this plant is not only delicious, it is quite nutritious as well. Although the plant is well-armed with stinging hairs that can inflict quite a painful sensation on bare skin, the chemical responsible for the sting is rendered harmless by cooking. Once cooked, it turns to protein, making Nettles one of the highest-known sources of protein (about 7% by weight) in a leafy green vegetable.

The "sting" in Stinging Nettle is caused by formic acid (also found in ants), and other histamine-triggering substances. Unlike Poison Ivy, where the skin irritation usually doesn't show up for 24-48 hours but can last for two weeks or more, Stinging Nettle's impact is more immediate but relatively short in duration. The sting is felt almost immediately, but its worst effects fade in an hour or so and rarely last more than a day. If even that seems too much to bear, you may want to find some Curled Dock (*Rumex crispus*), Stinging Nettle's best known antidote and eminently edible in its own right- see page 66. Fortunately, the plants often grow in close proximity to each other. Just crush and rub the Curled Dock leaves in the affected area, and the effect may be enhanced if you repeat the phrase developed in England for this purpose: "Nettle in, Dock out."

Nettles tend to grow in patches of 100 plants or more, in bright sun or partial shade. They prefer rich, loamy soil such as that found along the edges of pastures and farm buildings. (The English have another saying, "Plant a fruit tree where Nettles grow," because of the trees' similar fondness for rich soil.) Nettle flowers and seeds are small, greenish and very inconspicuous. Their size and growing habit resembles that of the unrelated but equally edible Mint Family, especially Catnip (*Nepeta cataria*, see page 65), but the Nettles' sting is a dead giveaway.

Nettles are most edible soon after they come up in mid-April, earlier than most spring greens. Nettles are tastiest when young, a foot or less in height. If you miss them at this stage, you can still pick the tender tops from the taller plants for a few more weeks. They will eventually grow to about 3-4 feet in height. Occasionally, young and tender plants can be found in the fall, but in nowhere near the profusion as in spring. If you miss the tender stages, take note of where the Nettles grow; they are perennials, and will come back in the same spot the following season. Don't forget to harvest Nettles with gloves or some other hand protection, as even young plants can sting fiercely. Snip Nettle tops off with a pair of scissors in one hand, and then stuff them into a collecting bag with your other hand.

Stinging Nettle at the harvesting

Of course, it is necessary to cook Nettles before eating them. Though many wild greens are reputed to taste like spinach, including Chickweed (*Stellaria media*), tender Mulberry leaves and shoots (*Morus spp.*), and Lambs Quarters (*Chenopodium album*) (all of which are discussed in Part Four), Nettle greens have a flavor more reminiscent of split peas. Nettles contain a lot of protein, as well as many other vitamins and minerals including Vitamins A, B, C, iron, calcium and potassium.

Cooked Nettles can be eaten right away or frozen for later use. The best way to cook Nettles is first to wash them thoroughly in a large pot of cold water. Next, use tongs to throw the washed greens into a saucepan with the water still clinging to them from the washing process. Using only this water, steam them for about five minutes, and *voilà*! At this point the steamed Nettle greens are ready to be eaten as is or incorporated into a host of other dishes. (Some people also like to save the greenish cooking water (called "pot likker") for drinking as is or for use as soup stock.) Nettles are also good in soup (see below), quiche, spanikopita (also see below), and any other recipe calling for cooked spinach.

Stinging Nettle is also highly thought of as a medicinal plant. As one might deduce from the plant's prickly nature, Stinging Nettle is employed in homeopathic remedies to build up the body's resistance to inflammation. Naturopathic physicians consider freeze-dried Stinging Nettle to be an effective remedy for hay fever.

Last but not least, Stinging Nettle may not be bad for your outside after all. Nettles' former use as a fiber source for fabric appears to be making a comeback. Clothing was made from Nettles as long as 2,000 years ago, but lost its popularity when cotton arrived in the 16th century, which was easier to harvest and spin. Nettles made a brief comeback during World War I, when Germany suffered a shortage of cotton and Nettles were used to produce German army uniforms. The renewed interest in Stinging Nettle fiber is being driven by concern over the environmental damage caused by the production process for cotton which accounts for nearly one-quarter of all pesticide use worldwide. In the hunt for new, ecologically friendly fabrics, Stinging Nettle fiber shows great promise. Not only do Nettles require little if any pesticide use, but the fabric made from Nettles is softer and silkier than that made from flax or hemp fiber.

CREAM OF STINGING NETTLE SOUP (adapted from Phillips, *Wild Food*)

Cream of Stinging Nettle Soup may sound like something Morticia might have served on the old Addams Family 1960s TV show, but it's actually quite delicious and very easy to prepare.

INGREDIENTS:

2 cups (at least) steamed Nettle greens (fresh or previously frozen)
1 large onion
1 clove garlic
2 medium-sized potatoes (OK to substitute Jerusalem Artichoke- see Chapter Thirteen)
2 Tbsp olive oil
4 cups homemade chicken stock or canned chicken broth (diluted)

Cream of Stinging Nettle soup.

Salt and pepper to taste (OK to substitute dried, crushed Spicebush berries for the black pepper, see Chapters Three and Eight)
1/2 cup Half-and-Half
2 slices bread, cubed
1-2 Tbsp butter

PREPARATION:

Peel and finely chop the onion, garlic and potatoes and fry them in the olive oil 3-4 minutes in a large pot or saucepan. In the meantime, heat the chicken stock to the boiling point. Add stock to the vegetables in a saucepan and boil fairly rapidly for 15 minutes or until the potatoes have cooked. Add the Nettle greens to the pot, mix well, and liquify the mixture in a blender. Pour the puréed mixture back into the pot to reheat and season with salt and pepper. Pour into a large bowl when ready to serve and stir in the half and half. Serve with croutons made by sautéing bread cubes in butter.

WILD GREENS SPANIKOPITA

INGREDIENTS:

Wild Greens Spanikopita

1 cup chopped wild onion (*Allium canadensis*) bulbs (OK to substitue cultivated onions)
4 cups (at least) steamed Stinging Nettle greens (or 6 cups of well-washed raw Lambs Quarters (*Chenopodium album*),Galinsoga (*Galinsoga parviflora*) Chickweed (*Stellaria media*) or other mild greens, which do not need to be pre-cooked. Stronger greens such as Curled Dock (*Rumex crispus*), Sow Thistle (*Sonchus oleraceus*), Dandelion (*Taraxacum officinale*) or Field Mustard (*Brassica campestris*) can be added or substituted for a stronger bite, but you may want to parboil them a minute or two first.
2 Tbsp olive oil
1 cup feta cheese (substitute ricotta or cottage, if you must)
2 eggs
2 Tbsp parsley
2 Tbsp chopped wild chives (OK to substitute cultivated chives)
Salt and pepper to taste
12 phyllo (filo) pastry leaves (most supermarkets and Mediterranean food stores sell it — look for it in the refrigerator or freezer case)
1/4 cup melted butter or margarine

PREPARATION:

Sauté the onions in the olive oil in a large skillet; add the fresh greens; cover and cook 5 minutes or until the greens are wilted and tender. If you are using pre-cooked greens, add them along with the other ingredients after you have sautéed the onions. Add cheese, eggs, parsley, wild chives, salt and pepper, mix in well, and then cool slightly. Cut phyllo leaves to make 24 sheets; layer the first 12 sheets in a well-greased baking dish (6" X 10" or equivalent), brushing each layer with the melted butter or margarine (a pastry brush is useful here). Spoon the cooked mixture into the baking dish and spread evenly over the phyllo. Cover with the remaining phyllo, brushing each layer with butter. Bake at 350º for 1 hour or until golden.
Serves 6-8 people.

CHAPTER TWO

JAPANESE KNOTWEED: IF YOU CAN'T BEAT IT, EAT IT

Japanese Knotweed

Although sometimes referred to as "Mexican Bamboo" (a name that doesn't really fit as the plant is neither Mexican nor a true Bamboo), this plant is better known as Japanese Knotweed (*Polygonum cuspidatum*, or *Reynoutria* or *Fallopia japonica*).

Japanese Knotweed is despised among the gardening and ecology set for its steadfast refusal to give ground once it is established. Botanists seeking to safeguard the habitat of indigenous flora have labeled it an "aggressive alien invader." In fact, the plant does present a serious threat to rare species habitat, particularly along northern rivers whose banks and bars are scoured by ice each spring.

Although some attempts have been made to control Japanese Knotweed mechanically (e.g., by repeatedly chopping down the plants' stems to sap its strength, a method that is compatible with harvesting the plant for food), people are increasingly resorting to spraying the plant stalks with herbicide. If you see a knotweed patch with discolored and/or flaccid stalks, you should strongly suspect that it has been sprayed and look for a unaffected patch from which to harvest (which shouldn't be too hard to find).

The person thought to be responsible for bringing Japanese Knotweed into the United States was none other than Frederic Law Olmsted, the eminent landscape architect and designer of Boston's Emerald Necklace park system. (This might help to explain why the plant is so abundant in that particular area.) Olmsted probably brought the plant here from England in the nineteenth century as an ornamental. To an unjaundiced eye, Japanese Knotweed is attractive, with a late-blooming, foamy mass of white flowers, followed by a persistent clump of dried stalks and seeds of an unusual, reddish-brown color. Needless to say, if Olmsted had known about the plant's aggressive habits, he might have had second thoughts.

Although Japanese Knotweed does bear a superficial resemblance to Bamboo — especially when its hollow stalks turn brown at the end of the growing season — it is actually a member of the Polygonaceae or Buckwheat Family, which includes the edible wild plants Sheep Sorrel (*Rumex acetosella*), Curled Dock (*Rumex crispus*) (see pages 71 and 66), and the cultivated plant Rhubarb, to which Japanese Knotweed's flavor is most often compared.

"Polygonum" means "many knees" in Greek, and refers to the joint-like swellings every six inches or so along its stalk, which are usually covered in part by a papery sheath. The plant is a relatively late bloomer, producing panicles of small, cream-colored blossoms in mid to late summer, followed 1-2 months later by clusters of brown, papery seeds.

Japanese Knotweed prefers disturbed areas such as roadsides and railroad tracks, but can also be found along relatively pristine streambanks, especially those that have been disturbed by ice scour. The plants typically grow in dense patches, 12 or more feet in diameter and six feet or more in height. When you locate a mature patch, take note of its whereabouts; although the plant is an herbaceous perennial (which means the above-ground part of the plant dies back at the end of each growing season), the dried stalks typically persist through the winter and make it easy to locate the clumps of new shoots the following spring.

Japanese Knotweed shoots usually make their first appearance in mid-April, a week or two after Stinging Nettle. The same aggressive growing habits gardeners and ecologists dislike are a boon to foragers, as the plant is prolific enough to support repeated harvesting, and it only takes a few minutes to gather all you need.

Perhaps gardeners and ecologists might see the plant in a slightly more charitable light if they were aware of its considerable culinary value. Japanese Knotweed shoots at the "Asparagus" stage are green, flecked with red, about a foot tall, and tender and mild in flavor. They take less time than asparagus to cook (steam them only 2-3 minutes). One fancy restaurant in Montpelier, Vermont, specializes in wild foods and sells steamed Japanese Knotweed shoots as "Red Asparagus," charging diners $4 a plate for it. Steamed Knotweed tends to be on the mucilaginous side, so you might want to add some bread crumbs to sop up the juice. Cooked shoots are also good served chilled and with salad dressing. Puréed Knotweed also makes and excellent base for "fruit" soup, especially when the juice of tarter and redder fruit such as Barberry (*Berberis vulgaris*, see Chapter Fourteen) is added to enhance its color and flavor.

By early May, the Knotweed shoots become young stalks about 1-2 feet high. To harvest, select the fattest stalks you find (usually 3/4 to 1 inch in diameter), slide your hand down the stalk until it feels woody, chop it off above that point and then lop the unfolding, spade-shaped leaves off the top. If you are lucky, you may discover a patch of the less common Giant Knotweed (*Polygonum sachalinense*), the "3-D Drive-in movie" cousin of Japanese Knotweed, which is larger in every respect, making the stalks easier to peel. (Japanese and Giant Knotweed are also known to hybridize.)

The tender green insides of the hollow Knotweed stalks are tart and juicy, similar in flavor to a Granny Smith apple. They are fun to eat right on the spot, or you can take the stalks home, peel the stringy outside layer off and use the tender core as a raw material for any recipe calling for Rhubarb. (Be careful not to peel too deeply, however, or all that will be left is the hole!) Peeled Knotweed stalks make an excellent Strawberry-Knotweed pie, which is arguably much tastier than Strawberry-Rhubarb Pie (see recipe below or just follow your preferred recipe for Strawberry-Rhubarb Pie, substituting an equivalent amount of peeled Knotweed stalks for the Rhubarb). Do be aware, however, that some people find Japanese Knotweed (like Rhubarb) to be slightly laxative.

Last but not least, it appears that eating Japanese Knotweed may lower your risk of heart attack. The plant contains resveratrol, a heart-healthy substance that has also been found in grape skins and leaves. Two "60 Minutes" stories in the 1990s cxamined why the French, who have relatively high-fat diets, don't suffer more heart attacks. One of the plausible explanations was that they typically consume red wine with every meal. (White wine does not include the resveratrol-containing grape skins.) Apparently, the Japanese have known about Knotweed's beneficial effect for centuries, and have used it as a traditional treatment for cardiovascular disease. Resveratrol is also reputed to have some effectiveness against herpes as well as inhibiting the growth of cancer tumors. While resveratrol is also found in peanuts and Mulberries (see page 69), Japanese Knotweed roots are the commercial source of resveratrol for the herbal supplement market.

STRAWBERRY KNOTWEED PIE

I get a lot of compliments on this pie, which I gratefully receive, but I really should share the credit with someone else. I learned the art of pie-making from my mother, Rhoda Rudman Cohen, who herself learned how to make pies during her childhood in Maine. My mother kindly gave me permission to share with you some of her pie-making secrets, some of which have been updated for modern kitchens. One of the secrets which I'm sure many of you already know is to use lard as part of the shortening to get a nice, flaky crust. If you would rather not use lard, you can substitute butter or another shortening (but don't expect to get as good results). This recipe works equally well for Juneberry, Black Raspberry, Mulberry and any other fruit pie.

To make pie dough (for a 9" diameter pie plate):

INGREDIENTS::

> Exactly 1 2/3 cup white flour
> 5 Tbsp butter (should be cold)
> 5 Tbsp vegetable shortening or lard
> (should be cold)
> 7 Tbsp cold apple or orange juice
> Wax paper

PREPARATION:

Pour flour into a food processor. Cut up shortening into big pieces and add to food processor- the less handling the better. Pulse until coarsely chopped (small lumps are OK). Add cold juice to mixture and pulse until it begins to ball up and the blade stops or slows

Strawberry Knotweed pie and shoot at the "Wild Rhubarb" stage.

down substantially. Dump contents onto a piece of wax paper; shape into a ball and place in the refrigerator to chill for at least one hour.

25

To make pie:

> 1 cup sugar
> 3+ cups sliced strawberries
> 3+ cups peeled, sliced Japanese Knotweed stalks (cut each Knotweed stalk piece in half length-wise to reduce any trapped air space inside).
> 1/2 tsp ground nutmeg
> 1 tsp ground cinnamon
> 1/2 tsp ground allspice

Preparation:

Preheat oven to 425º. Remove chilled dough ball from the refrigerator, cut in half and slap one of the halves onto a large, floured breadboard. Spread the dough with the base of your hand, then use a rolling pin to spread it out more, adding flour to the pin, board and/or dough if they get sticky. Flip dough over occasionally. Spread the dough into a circle about 1/8" thick, then fold it in half, place in bottom of pie plate and unfold. Mix the filling ingredients together in a bowl; if runny juice accumulates on the bottom of the bowl, stir a tablespoon or so of flour into the filling mixture to help absorb it. Pour the filling into the pie plate. Repeat the process with the second dough ball half, and use this dough to cover filling (or cut into 1/2" strips and place over filling in lattice pattern) - trim off all but 1/2" surplus dough from pie plate rim. Crimp dough together along pie plate edge with a fork, fingers or other decorative technique, and trim off remaining excess dough on sides. Sprinkle a little water and sugar over the top and brush or blow off the excess. Using a fork, poke 6-12 holes in the top crust (if it is not a lattice type). Place on a cookie sheet and insert into the center rack of the oven. Bake for 20 minutes at 425º, then 25 minutes more at 400º. Pie is done when juice oozes out the top crust and begins to run on to the cookie sheet. Note: If the crust is getting too brown in one or more places before the rest is done, place a small piece of aluminum foil over that spot to retard further browning.

Strawberry-Knotweed pies can be frozen in their raw state; just give them a day or two to thaw in the refrigerator before you bake them. The crusts of previously-frozen pies have a tendency to overcook, however, so cover the whole outer crust edge in aluminum foil after the first five minutes in the oven and leave in place until the last ten minutes of baking.

CHAPTER THREE

SASSAFRAS: TREASURED BY EXPLORERS AND CHEFS

Sassafras (*Sassafras albidum*) is a native plant that is relatively common in Southern New England, especially near the coast. Although the trees can get to be 30 feet or more in height (e.g., on Nantucket) Sassafras typically tends to be on the small, spindly side in Essex County. Sassafras is one of the easiest trees to identify because of its distinctive mitten-shaped leaves. Leaves with no "thumbs," one "thumb" and two "thumbs" are typically found on each tree.

Most parts of the Sassafras plant contain aromatic oils. Sassafras' aromatic character seems to be a common trait in the Lauraceae or Laurel Family, which Sassafras shares with such estimable culinary stalwarts as cinnamon, bay leaves and avocado. (Mountain Laurel (*Kalmia latifolia*), a poisonous plant, is not in this family.) Spicebush (*Lindera benzoin*), another native American edible wild plant, is also related to Sassafras. True to form, Spicebush has aromatic bark (its twigs can be steeped for a backwoods tea), and bright red berries that, when dried and ground, make a fine substitute for Szechuan peppercorns (see Milkweed Egg Puff recipe, Chapter Eight).

Native Americans used Sassafras extensively for flavoring as well as medicinally. Sassafras was also a very common flavoring for patent and other medicines before the mid-1900s. Along with Groundnut (see Chapter Five), Sassafras was one of the plants that early explorers presented with great fanfare in the royal courts of Europe when they returned from their first forays to the New World. They extolled the plants' virtues in an attempt to justify the huge sums the monarchs had shelled out to support the expeditions. In the early 1600s, Sassafras tea was believed to cure a host of ailments, and a number of tea houses sprung up to meet a growing demand. But when Sassafras tea developed a reputation as a cure for Syphilis, its use in public dropped off precipitously.

The outer bark of Sassafras roots has a distinctive and easily recognizable "root beer" aroma. Sassafras was at one time a major flavoring ingredient in commercial root beer. Some years ago, the Food and Drug Administration determined that safrole, one of the substances contained in the aromatic oil of Sassafras roots, is carcinogenic, and consequently banned the roots' use in certain situations. This action has since been called into question, especially since subsequent studies showed that safrole is carcinogenic to rats but not to people, and that the safrole in a 12-ounce can of naturally flavored Sassafras root beer is less than one-tenth as carcinogenic as is the ethanol in a 12-ounce can of beer. Note also that cinnamon and nutmeg, which contain significant amounts of safrole, have not been banned. Nevertheless, you may want to hedge your bets by consuming items made from Sassafras roots on an occasional rather than frequent basis.

Sassafras roots make an excellent root beer-flavored tea. To make your own, simply peel the bark off the roots or just chop up the roots and simmer in water for a half hour or so for a delicious, naturally sweet tea. Sassafras roots can be reused several times before losing their potency. You can also make excellent candy from Sassafras, as the recipe below will attest.

Sassafras leaves

The young twigs and leaves of the Sassafras plant contain a different aromatic oil with an equally pleasant "lemony" flavor, which has been compared to Froot Loops™ cereal. Young Sassafras leaves are edible raw or cooked. (The safrole content in the leaves is negligible.) They have a mucilaginous, "okra-like" quality that is well-suited to thickening and flavoring soups and stews. Did you know that filé powder, used extensively in Creole cooking (Filé Gumbo, for example), is nothing other than dried, powdered sassafras leaves? In some restaurants in New Orleans, each table contains a shaker of filé powder next to the salt, pepper and Tabasco sauce. To make filé powder, pick young leaves up to one and a half inches long, dry thoroughly (a food dehydrator is not needed), pulverize by hand or in a food processor, sift out any fibrous bits, and then store in a jar until ready to use.

Sassafras is typically found growing in dry, deciduous woodlands as a spindly understory tree that reaches from 6-12 feet in height. The trees often grow in patches of 20 or more. To harvest the root, grab one of the smaller trees near the base and give it a strong, steady tug— you will usually get about a foot's length of root, more than enough to flavor several batches of tea. A new tree will usually sprout from the portion of the root remaining in the ground. (Nevertheless, check to make sure there are at least a dozen other Sassafras plants around before pulling one up.) The roots are harvestable and useable year-round; the young leaves are available in mid-spring and in decreasing quantity until early summer.

Sassafras is also fun to look for in winter. Its green twigs stand out among the otherwise darker and drabber dormant vegetation. Just "scratch and sniff" some of the twig bark and if you get a fragrant, fruity odor, you've found it. Sassafras' cousin Spicebush is also relatively easy to spot in the winter for its unusual spherical green leaf buds; it also performs well in the "scratch and sniff" test.

SASSAFRAS CANDY

This candy may awaken pleasant childhood memories of buying root beer barrels at the penny candy store. It can be made year-round, either by using previously harvested frozen roots or by digging a fresh supply of roots. The key to making an intense-flavored Sassafras candy is to add the root pieces after the liquid is heated to the "hard crack" candy stage; otherwise the volatile oil containing the flavor will be driven off.

You will need a candy thermometer for this recipe

INGREDIENTS:

> 1/2 cup or more of Sassafras root bark (i.e., the peeled root from
> approximately 24 inches worth of root pieces)
> 2 cups water
> 4 cups sugar
> 1 1/4 cups light corn syrup
> 1 Tbsp butter or margarine
> One well-buttered large baking dish or cookie sheet with
> a rim of 1/2 inch or more.

PREPARATION:

Lightly scrub roots in cold water to remove any residual dirt, then peel the bark off the root pieces with a knife or carrot peeler. Bring the water to a low boil. (Optional: throw the peeled roots in and simmer for a while to give the water a little preliminary flavor and color boost.) Put the peeled root bark in a food processor and pulverize until it is coarsely ground. You should have at least 1/2 cup of pulverized bark pieces when finished (less will result in a less intense flavor). Remove root pieces from the simmering water and add the remaining ingredients to the liquid. Boil at a high temperature and insert candy thermometer. When the boiling liquid approaches a temperature of between 290-300°, stir in the pulverized root bark and mix well. The mixture will sizzle and drop in temperature about 20-30 degrees as the moisture in the root bark boils off. When the temperature of the mixture gets back up to between 300-310° (the so-called "hard crack" stage), remove from heat and spread the mixture evenly in the baking dish or cookie sheet. As the candy begins to solidify, score its surface with a knife to help break it into uniform pieces later. Store whatever you don't eat right away in tightly sealed glass jars in a cool place, and it should retain its flavor and hardness for a year or more.

CHAPTER FOUR

BLACK LOCUST: FINE FOR FRITTERS AND FENCE POSTS

Black Locust

Black Locust (*Robinia pseudoacacia*) is a tree with deeply furrowed bark that typically grows up to 60 feet in height. The tree has bluish-green compound leaves with 11 or so egg-shaped leaflets. The twigs and smaller branches (and occasionally even the trunks) have thorns. These are easily avoided when harvesting. Black Locust is native to the Southeast states and was introduced to the Northeast in part because its rot-resistant wood was popular for fence posts. Now commonly found along roadsides and field edges, it has the dubious distinction of being one of the featured plants on several invasive plant species lists for the region.

The only edible part of Black Locust is the flower; the remainder (leaves, seeds, roots, bark, etc.) is poisonous. When the flowers are in bloom, the air fills with their sweet, jasmine-like fragrance, so that sometimes you can smell it on a warm spring evening while biking or driving with the windows down.

Black Locust flowers are harvestable for two or three weeks around Memorial Day. To harvest, find a tree with reachable flowering branches (this is usually not too difficult). The white flowers hang in clusters (called racemes), about a dozen or so per cluster. Each individual blossom has the familiar "wing and keel" structure of flowers in the Pea family (Fabaceae). Sniff each flower cluster before putting it in your bag; if you get a strong sweet smell, then it's a "keeper"; if there is little or no smell, the flowers have passed their prime for eating and you should leave them be. Usually, the flower

Black Locust flowers

clusters that have a couple of unopened buds at the outer end contain the best fragrance and flavor. (A tip for you procrastinators out there: if you have just missed the harvesting season in your neighborhood, head north— into Southern New Hampshire if need be—and catch up with the plants where the growing season starts later.)

The flowers are delicious raw, with a flavor similar to pea pods dipped in honey. Simply strip them off the central stalk and toss them into a salad. The flowers are also delicious in

Black Locust Fritters (see recipe below). This is the kind of dish you can impress company with by serving for Sunday Brunch. Fritters made from previously frozen flowers are just as (if not more) tasty as those made from fresh flowers.

BLACK LOCUST FRITTERS

INGREDIENTS:

2 cups Black Locust flowers
(raw or frozen)
2 eggs, separated
1 Tbsp melted butter
2/3 cup milk
1 cup all-purpose flour
1/4 teaspoon salt
1 Tbsp granulated sugar
1/2 cup orange juice
confectioner's sugar

Black Locust fritters surrounded by blossoms.

PREPARATION:

Beat together egg yolks, melted butter and milk in a bowl. In a separate bowl, mix together flour, salt and granulated sugar. Combine all ingredients; cover, and allow to sit at least two hours in the refrigerator (overnight is OK). Remove from refrigerator and beat well until smooth. Whip the two egg whites until they are stiff and gently fold them into the batter. Add about 2 cups of the Black Locust flowers (stripped off their central stalks first) and mix until blended. (If using frozen flowers, it is not necessary for them to thaw first.) Fill a large skillet with cooking oil about 1/4" deep, and turn stove on to a medium-high heat (about the same temperature you would cook omelettes or pancakes). Once the oil is hot, drop in large spoonfuls of the fritter batter and fry for a minute or two on each side until they are golden brown. Remove and pat dry with a paper towel; squeeze a little orange juice on each fritter, dust with confectioner's sugar, and serve while warm. Leftover fritters can be frozen and reheated in a toaster oven.

Makes about 15 fritters

CHAPTER FIVE

GROUNDNUT: THE PILGRIMS WOULDN'T HAVE PROGRESSED WITHOUT IT

Groundnut

The above-ground part of the Groundnut (*Apios americana*) plant is a vine, with bean-like compound leaves, each composed of 5-7 leaflets. These rarely get more than five feet off the ground, twining around any available support (note the lack of tendrils). In mid-summer, Groundnut vines develop clusters of fragrant, chocolate-colored blossoms that resemble those of garden peas or beans (which is not surprising, as Groundnut is a member of the same botanical family, the Fabaceae). The flowers are eventually followed by pods containing edible beans. (I can't tell you whether or not they are worth eating, as I have only found them a few times, and keep forgetting to try eating them.)

From an alimentary standpoint, the most important part of the plant lies below the ground. The tubers typically lie 2-3" below the surface, and range in size from a marble to larger than a golf ball.

Groundnut tubers played a crucial role in the original European settlement of New England. Although you may have been taught otherwise in grammar school, it was these tubers, not corn, that kept the Pilgrims alive during the harsh winter of 1620-21, their first in the New World. In fact, Groundnut tubers were so important to the early colonists that many felt the need to pass ordinances forbidding Indians from harvesting them from Colonial settlements. In Essex County, one of these settlements was the Town of Ipswich (then called Agawam). Groundnuts were subsequently transported back to Europe where attempts were made to domesticate them, but to no avail.

Groundnut plants like to grow in damp, sandy, alluvial soil such as that found in river floodplains. The tubers are spaced about 3" apart along a string-like root. They are harvestable any time the ground isn't frozen, although during the colder months it takes some skill to locate the beige-colored dead vines still clinging to their former means of support. A case in point: some time ago, I went on a cross-country skiing trip to central Vermont sponsored by the Appalachian Mountain Club. It was one of those winters where the skiing conditions were excellent at the higher elevations, but at lower elevations (where we were) the ground was bare and not even frozen. While walking one early morning, I noticed some familiar-looking dried vines on a trail along a river. I dug a test hole and, sure enough, came up with a Groundnut tuber. I quickly dug up a dozen more, and we had them with our breakfast that morning.

Harvesting the tubers usually involves some digging. You may, however, have the same luck I had one spring while canoeing along the Contoocook River in central New Hampshire. The river had recently flooded, washing away a layer of topsoil and exposing the Groundnut tuber strings. All I had to do was bend down and pick them up.

Groundnut tubers

Harvested Groundnut tubers will keep in the refrigerator for a month or so. Wrap them in slightly moistened paper towels or freeze them. The tubers are high in starch and protein and, although edible raw, they are much better cooked. (Sliced raw tubers ooze a milky sap, which is not noticible after cooking.) The best way to prepare Groundnuts is simply to slice them thinly crosswise (no need to peel them) and fry them in vegetable oil in a skillet until golden, then dry them with a paper towel, lightly salt and serve promptly. If you wait too long, the chips lose much of their crispness and flavor. Groundnut tubers can also be baked like potatoes.

One last cautionary note about Groundnut: Groundnuts, which are related to peanuts, may cause an allergic reaction in some people who eat them.

CHAPTER SIX

CATTAIL: WORTH GETTING YOUR FEET WET FOR

Most people can look across an open marshy area and recognize Cattails (*Typha latifolia* and *angustifolia*). This familiar plant often grows in solid stands, its bluish-green 4-5-foot leaves arising from the base of each plant. Many Cattails develop a brown seedhead that looks just like a hot dog on a stick. Although the "hot dog" isn't edible, most of the rest of the plant is. Indeed, Euell Gibbons, wild foods guru of the '60s and '70s, dubbed the Cattail the "Supermarket of the Swamps" for its many edible parts. Although at least two of these parts are available year-round, I tend to think of harvesting Cattails in June when the bloom spikes are in season. But before getting to them, let me tell you about the other parts.

There are three edible portions of the cattail at or below ground level. Attached at or near the base of most Cattail stalks (alive or dead) is a small white pointed sprout about 1/3" to 5/8" in diameter and ranging from 1" to 4" long. This is the leading shoot for next year's Cattail stalk. These are available year-round and can be chopped into salads or steamed and eaten like Brussels sprouts (but, unlike Brussels sprouts, they have a mild, cucumber-like flavor). Inside the base of each live Cattail stalk you will find a lump of starchy tissue (about an inch in diameter) that can be roasted and eaten like potatoes. These are available in spring and into summer.

Cattail rhizomes are ropy, cylindrical roots, usually more than 1/2" thick, which run horizontally just below the surface, and often connect adjacent Cattail plants. Rhizomes store energy in the form of starch to help the developing shoots and stalks in the spring. These rhizomes can be harvested and the starch extracted to make a very acceptable flour substitute.

In the typical Cattail marsh, the stalks and rhizomes are packed quite close together; digging for the rhizomes can (but needn't) be back-breaking work. The most efficient way to harvest Cattail is to paddle out to the upper reaches of tidal creeks, such as those feeding into Plum Island Sound. Time your trip so that you arrive halfway between low- and high tide, and then harvest the Cattail rhizomes you see sticking out of the muddy banks. Break off as much as you can, rinse it off in the creek and toss it into your boat. Although Cattail rhizomes can be harvested year-round, the dormant season (October - April) is best as the rhizomes are especially packed with starch at that time.

Here's how to make Cattail flour: rinse off any remaining mud from the rhizomes. Peel the outer spongy part off each rhizome to expose the starchy inner core; immerse the cores in a bucket of fresh water and pull them apart with your hands to get the starch from the rhizome's internal fibers into the water. The starch will turn the water cloudy. Allow about an hour for the starch to settle. Pour off the water. Repeat the washing/settling process if necessary. This wet flour is now ready to use as is or dried for later use. You can substitute Cattail flour for up to half the total amount of flour in most conventional recipes, or you can develop your own recipes that use a higher percentage of Cattail flour. You can even try mixing in some Cattail pollen (see below).

Now for the edible portions of Cattails that are above-ground. Cattail hearts are simply the tender tissue at the inner core of the developing Cattail stalk. The hearts are found near the base of the plants when the stalks are 2-3 feet tall (usually the latter part of May in Essex County). Strip off the outer leaves until you reach the soft, whitish-to-yellowish green center. The hearts can be chopped into salads or used like scallions in cooked dishes. Like the sprouts, they have a mild, cucumber-like flavor.

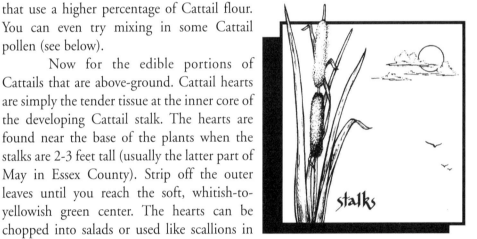

stalks

The next edible portion to develop is the immature Cattail flower or "bloom spike." These should be harvested just before they emerge from the top of the Cattail stalk (mid-to-late June in Essex County).

To harvest the immature Cattail flower, look for a slight swelling under the leaves near the top of the plant. Peel the leaves back and you will find two parts: a pale green female flower cluster on the bottom, topped by a dark green male flower cluster on top. The flesh of the male portion is more abundant and requires less cooking than the female. Nevertheless, the flesh on the female portion, although thin, is delicious. Boil or steam the bloom spikes for 15 minutes or so until tender (if you use the female flowers, start boiling them a couple minutes ahead of the male flowers). They tend to be a bit on the dry side, so try serving them with butter, Hollandaise or other sauce.

Cattail bloom spikes have a very pleasant, mild flavor, somewhat resembling corn with a hint of artichoke. The edible pulp remains attached to the stalk after cooking, so diners will typically strip the pulp off the spikes with their teeth and end up with a pile of what looks like plastic knitting needles when they are done. If you or any of your dinner guests have concerns about dental work, you can use a knife to strip the pulp off the cooked spikes before serving. The stripped pulp can also be incorporated into casseroles or other cooked dishes such as Cattail Chowder (see recipe below).

By the way, Cattail hearts are still available at this stage: the tender inner portion of the stalk merely migrates upward along with the developing bloom spike. Peel back the outer leaves surrounding the stalk to find a tender section of stalk several inches long. You can eat it on the spot, add it to salads or raita (an Indian yogurt sauce), or make excellent pickles with it. However, any tender parts inside the stalk disappear once the Cattail flowers are fully emerged.

The last edible part of the Cattail is the pollen. Once the bloom spikes emerge, the upper male flowers will take on a yellowish tinge as they begin to produce and release pollen. The best time and place to collect this pollen is on a dry, still morning when the flower tops are plainly visible. Wrap a medium-sized plastic bag around each bloom spike and give it a quick shake. This will release a bright yellow cloud of pollen that will eventually settle. If you time it right, you should easily be able to collect at least cup of pollen. Take what you've gathered home and pour it through a sifter or similar device to remove any impurities. This hypoallergenic pollen can now be added to flour to make nutritious and colorful Cattail pollen pancakes, cookies, muffins (see cover photo), etc. Freeze whatever you don't use in a day or two.

As if all of these edible parts aren't enough, Cattails have many other uses. The leaves are used for mats and rush seating; seedhead-tipped stalks are used for torches and flower-arranging; and the seedhead's fluffy material is used to stuff pillows, mattresses and life-preservers. It is no surprise that Cattails were and are so highly thought of by Native Americans.

One cautionary note: avoid harvesting the portions you intend to eat from patches whose cleanliness you think may be compromised by road runoff, landscaping/agricultural chemicals or other sources of contamination.

CATTAIL CHOWDER

INGREDIENTS:

> 8 ounces salt pork, diced (can substitute bacon,
> or for meatless version, use 3 Tbsp butter)
> 2 onions, chopped
> 1/2 cup celery and tops
> 1/2 bay leaf, crushed (OK to substitute one Bayberry
> (*Myrica pensylvanica*) leaf)
> 2 Tbsp all-purpose flour
> 2 cups water, chicken broth or seaweed stock (made from dried kelp –
> *Laminaria* or *Alaria spp.*)

3 cups diced potato (OK to substitute Jerusalem Artichoke tubers)
2 cups Cattail bloom spike pulp, stripped off the cores
(OK to substitute boiled cream-style corn)
2 cups whole milk or half-and-half
Salt and pepper to taste
2 Tbsp chopped parsley
Paprika

PREPARATION:

In large kettle, cook salt pork until brown and crisp. Remove pork and pour off all but three tablespoons of the fat (for meatless version, start by melting 3 tablespoons of butter in the kettle). Saute the onions in the fat/butter until just translucent, then add the Cattail bloom spike pulp, diced potato (or Jerusalem Artichoke tubers), Bay leaf and celery and sauté for another 4-5 minutes. Add and blend in the flour. Add water, broth or stock; bring to a low boil, and simmer, covered, for 15 minutes or until potatoes (or Jerusalem Artichokes) are tender. Reduce heat, add milk and/or half-and-half, and season to taste. Simmer, but do not to boil or it may curdle. Add pork/bacon if you are using it, then serve with parsley and paprika.

Chapter Seven

Pokeweed:
As American as Apple Pie (and just as tasty).

Pokeweed (*Phytolacca americana*) is an herbaceous perennial plant with succulent, thick stems and egg-shaped leaves. It is native to the United States (hence the species name *americana*). It typically reaches a height of 5-7 feet before dying back to the ground. Pokeweed is disliked by many who associate it with unkempt areas and highly disturbed ground such as piles of dirt, compost and wood chips. Yet, this delicious and highly attractive plant has been imported to Europe for its edible and ornamental value. Pokeweed is at its prettiest in late summer and into the fall, with its bright magenta-colored stems and clusters of large, shiny purple berries.

Fall is not the time to eat Pokeweed, however, as the entire plant at this stage is poisonous. The poison in Pokeweed is a purgative substance called phytolaccin. Although it has some proven therapeutic value in minute doses, ingesting too much phytolaccin will make everything on the inside of your body want to get to the outside through every available means as quickly as possible. The poison is present in all parts of the plant except for the young shoots, and is especially concentrated in the roots. But don't let these poisonous portions scare you; after all, many cultivated edible plants, such as potatoes and rhubarb, have poisonous parts as well.

Most serious foragers develop the ability to recognize edible wild plants out of season and memorize or record their locations, so that they can find and pick the plants at the right stage for harvesting. Pokeweed provides a good example of how this skill comes in handy. The easiest time to spot Pokeweed is in the fall when the mature plants are at their showiest; but Pokeweed is edible in the spring when the shoots are less than a foot tall and difficult to spot amidst surrounding vegetation. Fortunately, new shoots will usually emerge at or near the base of last year's now yellowish, dead and dry stalks.

Pokeweed is usually at the right state for picking in Essex County in mid- to late May. You can harvest as many shoots as you want and return for another crop a week or so later. The plant's stout taproot can easily produce several crops of shoots without losing any of its strength. Be careful not to harvest the poisonous root when harvesting the shoots. Also avoid any shoots that are already developing reddish stems, as they may also have phytolaccin in unsafe amounts.

Pokeweed shoots must be cooked before eating. Here is a good method: get a large pot of water boiling rapidly; add the Pokeweed shoots and boil hard for seven minutes. The boiling water will absorb any trace amount of phytolaccin from the shoots. Pour off and discard the water. The Pokeweed shoots are ready to eat as is, to be frozen for later use, or incorporated into other dishes. Pokeweed shoots are quite robust and will retain most of their size and firmness even after prolonged cooking. Boiled Pokeweed shoots make a fine substitute for asparagus and many other vegetables in a variety of recipes, as the following story will attest.

One recent Memorial Day weekend my wife Ellen and I went to Nantucket to visit some friends. As we rode our bikes from the ferry dock to their house, we passed over a newly-constructed section of bikeway. The disturbed earth within the right-of-way created prime habitat for a profusion of Pokeweed. The timing of our trip was just right, as most of the Pokeweed shoots were at a perfect stage for harvesting, and we were able to pick a large grocery bag full. As our friends were preoccupied with opening their cottage and caring for their young children, my wife and I prepared most of the meals, of which Pokeweed figured highly. One day we made Pokeweed Frittata (see recipe below) for breakfast, Cream of Pokeweed Soup for lunch, and Pasta Primavera with Pokeweed for dinner. The Pokeweed was delicious in all three dishes, and no one got tired of it.

Pokeweed shoots with the previous year's dried stalk.

Pokeweed is among the most well-known wild vegetables in the South, where the shoots are sold fresh and canned in supermarkets under the name "Poke Sallet" or "Poke Salad." Some of you might also remember a "Top 40" song from the late '60s by swamp-rocker Tony Joe White entitled, "Polk Salad Annie," in which the title character Annie cooks up a "mess" of Pokeweed shoots to supplement her family's meager food supply. As Pokeweed shoots reputedly are quite high in Vitamins C and A even after cooking, Annie's family had a healthy and cheap means of sustenance.

A few final notes of interest: the origin of the name "poke" is not, as you might think, from the edible shoots as they "poke" out of the ground; it is derived from an Algonquin Indian word, "pokan," meaning "dye". This refers to the fact that many Native American tribes used the purple juice from the ripe Pokeweed berries to dye fabrics, baskets and other items. Pokeweed berry juice was also used by early American colonists as ink for quill pens; some famous documents in American history, including the Declaration of Independence and/or the U.S. Constitution, were written and/or signed in Pokeberry ink, and President James K. Polk's campaign buttons reputedly carried a Pokeweed image. Besides Inkberry, other former names for this plant include Pigeonberry, as the berries were a popular food for the now-extinct Passenger Pigeon.

POKEWEED FRITATTA

INGREDIENTS:

> 6 eggs
> 2 cups cooked Pokeweed shoots, cut into one-inch lengths
> 1 1/2 Tbsp olive oil
> 1 garlic clove, minced
> 1/4 cup grated parmesan cheese
> Salt, pepper and/or seasonings to taste
> 2 Tbsp bread crumbs (optional)

PREPARATION

Drop raw Pokeweed shoots into rapidly boiling water and boil hard for 7 minutes. Pour off cooking water. Coat the bottoms of two 10-inch omelet pans with a little olive oil. Beat the eggs in a bowl until blended; add the Pokeweed, parmesan cheese and seasonings. Sauté the minced garlic in the the second omelet pan at medium-high heat for about a minute; then pour in the egg mixture, swirl to smooth the top, and cook until the bottom is set and the top is still. Sprinkle the bread crumbs on top of the egg mixture while the egg cooks. Once the egg mixture is set (this should not take longer than a minute or two), fit the second omelet pan on top of the first (like a lid) and carefully flip the combined pans over so that the "lid" becomes the skillet which is heated to complete the cooking (this should take another minute or two). Transfer to a heated platter, cut into wedges and serve.

Note: Any combination of cooked Pokeweed and/or other cooked vegetables or sauteed wild mushrooms may be substituted for the 2 cups of cooked Pokeweed in this recipe. If you don't have two omelet pans, you can cook the frittata in a cast iron or other oven-proof skillet and broil the top of the frittata in the oven until done instead of flipping it over.

CHAPTER EIGHT

MILKWEED: A PROCRASTINATING FORAGER'S DREAM FOOD

Common Milkweed (*Asclepias syriaca*) is an herbaceous perennial with unbranched stems typically reaching 3-4 feet in height. Its oblong leaves average 5-6" long and 2-4" wide and are borne in opposite pairs on the stalk. True to its name, the entire plant contains a milky-white latex. Common Milkweed is typically found in gardens, old fields, meadows, pastures and along roads and fences.

The species name for Common Milkweed, "syriaca," means "of Syria." This is misleading, as it is a native American plant. The name Common Milkweed is used to distinguish it from its less common (and inedible) cousins, Butterflyweed (*Asclepias tuberosa*) and Swamp Milkweed (*Asclepias incarnata*), which tend to be rarer and thus of limited suitability for harvesting anyway. Distinguishing characteristics of Common Milkweed are that it is the only one you will find in an open, dry field in a large-sized colony of hundreds of plants or more. Another way to tell Common Milkweed from Butterflyweed is that Butterflyweed juice is clear. From here on, Common Milkweed will simply be referred to as Milkweed.

Perhaps you have pleasant childhood memories of collecting Milkweed. In simpler times a favorite after-school pastime was to explore the local fields and woods in search of Mother Nature's subtle handiwork. One of the more memorable of these childhood outdoor experiences was encountering a patch of Milkweed with the ripe pods slit down the side and the flossy insides showing. What fun it was to split the pods wide open, throw their contents into the air, and watch their little gossamer parachutes sail off in the wind, to the consternation of farmers and landscapers everywhere.

What you might not have known until now is Milkweed's estimable culinary properties. Besides being tasty and abundant, at least four different parts of the plant

are edible at various times, providing multiple harvesting opportunities. In chronological order, the four edible parts of Milkweed are: the young shoots; the cluster of tender leaves at the top of the older shoots; the young flower buds; and the young seed pods.

Milkweed shoots (leaves and stems) are edible from the time they first emerge from the ground until they get about eight or so inches tall. This typically occurs in Essex County from mid- to late May. Once the shoots get beyond this height, the lower portion of the stems become too tough to eat, but you can still harvest the cluster of tender, younger leaves and stem tips from these older shoots.

It is important to note that at the shoot stage Milkweed has a poisonous look-alike called Spreading Dogbane (*Apocynum cannabinum*). Like Milkweed, Spreading Dogbane shoots have single stems and opposite leaves (although the stems and leaves tend to be more slender than Milkweed). Spreading Dogbane also has milky juice and a similar preference for old-field habitat. Dogbane shoots are always much thinner than those of Milkweed, and they are usally reddish-purple on the upper part of the stem. Milkweed stems and leaves are green and minutely fuzzy, while dogbane stems are smooth. By the time the respective plants reach the flower bud stage they are very easy to tell apart: true to its name, Spreading Dogbane "spreads." That is, it branches out near the top into three or more skinny stems, while Milkweed almost invariably remains single-stemmed. Nevertheless, cautious foragers may want to wait until the flower bud stage or later to harvest Milkweed, when it is easily distinguishable from Spreading Dogbane.

Milkweed buds usually develop in Essex County in mid-to-late June. Harvest the buds while they are still in a tight green cluster similar to a broccoli floret, as they are less tasty once the little buds have begun to elongate on their stems. There is little need to worry about picking too many, as each plant will typically produce more buds to at least partially replace the ones you take. The buds you haven't picked will soon grow into loose clusters of mauve-colored flowers with a wonderful lilac-like fragrance.

Not long after the plants have finished blooming, seed pods will begin to develop at the base of the flower clusters. When the pods are up to 1 1/2" long and still firm to the touch (not springy or spongy), they make a great cooked vegetable, with a flavor and texture virtually indistinguishable from green beans. The pods are typically at the right stage for harvesting in Essex County around the latter half of July.

pods

All of the above-mentioned Milkweed parts should be boiled before eating to tenderize them (and remove a possible slight toxicity they may have in the raw state). Although just about every author I have read on this subject says that you must boil Milkweed in several changes of water in order to render it edible, I have found that once is all that is needed if you follow the following method: add the Milkweed to a pot of boiling water and boil hard for about seven minutes. Pour off the cooking water, and the plant is ready to be eaten as is, frozen for later use, or incorporated into just about anything you would use conventional vegetables for: soups, casseroles, omelettes, etc.. Milkweed buds make a particularly good topping for homemade pizza, and the young pods are excellent in curries. Like

Pokeweed, Milkweed won't shrink appreciably or get mushy even after all that boiling; in fact, it will turn a lovely bright green color.

Milkweed flowers reputedly are edible - they only need be parboiled a minute or so before they make a great addition to pancake batter or soups, stews, casseroles or other vegetable dishes. You can also eat the insides of small Milkweed pods without any cooking at all.

Monarch butterflies rely heavily if not exclusively upon Milkweed at several stages during their life cycle. In spring, after their long journey from Mexico to New England, female Monarchs lay a single, yellowish-white egg on the underside of Milkweed leaves. Once they hatch, the beautiful black, white and yellow-striped caterpillars feed exclusively on Milkweed leaves, thereby acquiring an intense bitter flavor that makes them unpalatable to most predators. The adult butterflies feed on the Milkweed flower nectar. To be sure to minimize any impact your foraging may have on the Monarch, leave the milkweed

Milkweed flower buds

Milkweed flower buds

shoots, young leaves and flower buds alone, and stick to harvesting the young pods, which do not play a significant role in the butterfly's various life stages.

As you might expect from such a versatile plant, Milkweed has a number of other proven and potential uses. Native Americans used Common Milkweed and its cousins medicinally (Asclepias was the Greek god of healing). During World War II, while overseas supplies of kapok were less reliable, the U.S. government recruited volunteers (many of whom were children) to gather Milkweed seed floss for stuffing soldiers' flight jackets and life preservers. Today, Milkweed floss is increasingly employed as a natural organic stuffing for small pillows. Also during during World War II a number of (apparently unsuccessful) experiments were undertaken to see if Milkweed's white latex could make an acceptable rubber substitute. Milkweed seeds and/or latex are also currently being looked at as a possible source of renewable hydrocarbon-based fuel.

MILKWEED EGG PUFF

This is a versatile recipe in that other Milkweed or other wild plant parts may be substituted for the Milkweed buds and it should still turn out very well. Wild mushrooms may be added as well.

INGREDIENTS:

Milkweed egg puff

10 eggs
1/2 cup flour
1 tsp baking powder
1/2 tsp salt
1 pint (2 cups) small-curd cottage cheese
4 cups (1 lb) shredded Monterey Jack cheese
(OK to substitute Pepper Jack)
1/2 cup (1/4 lb) butter or margarine, melted and cooled
12-16 oz (3/4-1 lb) cooked Milkweed (*Asclepias syriaca*) flower buds and/or other wild vegetables
10 dried, crushed Spicebush (*Lindera benzoin*) berries (a Szcchuan peppercorn-like seasoning; OK to substitute 1/2 tsp ground black pepper)

PREPARATION:

In a large bowl, beat eggs until slightly frothy and lemon-colored. Add flour, baking powder, salt, Spicebush berries, cottage cheese, Jack cheese and butter; mix until smooth. Stir in Milkweed buds. Pour egg mixture into a well-buttered 9" X 13" baking dish. Bake, uncovered, in a 350° oven for about 40-45 minutes or until top is browned and center appears firm. Serve immediately. Makes 8 servings. Any leftovers will keep for at least a few days or may be frozen and reheated.

CHAPTER NINE

JUNEBERRY:
PRIZED FOR PEMMICAN
AND PIE FILLING

Juneberry (*Amelanchier canadensis* and related species) is also known by several other common names, among which are Shadbush and Serviceberry. "Juneberry" logically refers to the berries, which are usually ripe for several weeks in June (1-2 months later at higher elevations and/or latitudes). The name "Shadbush" comes from the flowers, which ostensibly bloom around the time when the shad (an anadromous fish) swim upstream to spawn.

There are two explanations for the odd name, "Serviceberry." The first is that the flowering branches were brought into churches for Easter service decorations. The second and more morbid explanation is that, before the advent of hydraulic equipment, it was impossible to bury people during winter because the ground was too hard to dig. Blooming Serviceberry trees were a sign that the ground was now soft enough to conduct burial services.

Juneberry is a shrub or small tree typically about 12 feet high with small, finely-toothed leaves and smooth gray bark. You may notice faint white vertical stripes running along its slender trunk. Juneberries are typically found along lake shores, rivers and streams (which also helps explain the "Shadbush" appellation). Because of their early and attractive blossoms and fruits, Juneberry trees are popular among landscapers, so another place to look for them is among the shrub plantings in parks and other landscaped areas.

Like Pokeweed, the best time to locate a Juneberry tree differs from its prime harvesting time. Juneberry trees are at their most conspicuous when flowering, so take note of their location then, and then return at harvest time.

Juneberry flowers

Juneberry fruit ripens about six weeks after the five-petalled white flowers bloom. Juneberry fruits are similar in size and appearance to Highbush Blueberries, except that they are reddish-purple when ripe. Unfortunately, Juneberry fruits are frequently afflicted with a fungus (a variety of Cedar-Apple Rust (*Gymnosporangium spp.*)) that ruins all or part of each tree's annual production. Berries affected by the fungus are misshapen, don't ripen properly and/or are covered by growths. Although Juneberries are very common on Nantucket, I have yet to find any Juneberry trees on that island not affected by the fungus.

Juneberry fruit

If you are fortunate to find a Juneberry tree with fungus-free ripe fruit, you will discover that they taste like a cross between cherries and almonds (not surprising since all three are botanical cousins within the Rose Family (*Rosaceae*)). It's great fun just to stuff your face right by the tree, but if you have enough discipline to bring some home you will find that both fresh or dried Juneberries make excellent pies, muffins and other baked goods (see recipe below). They are a bit on the bland side, however, and are probably best when blended with a tarter fruit — such as Red Mulberry (*Morus rubra*) and Black Raspberry (*Rubus occidentalis*) — which ripen around the same time. Juneberries also dry easily, and dried berries keep well even at room temperature if placed in a sealed glass container. Dried Juneberries make an excellent granola ingredient (see recipe below).

Native Americans made extensive use of Juneberries for Pemmican, their equivalent of Power Bars™. The berries were usually dried first in the sun and then pounded together with dried meat, nuts and melted fat. Pemmican was easily transportable and provided valuable sustenance for long journeys. A number of wildlife species, especially songbirds, also eat Juneberries. To assuage any guilty feelings you might have about possibly depriving them of a food supply, know that the typical Juneberry tree has plenty of berries that are too high to reach, thus ensuring that there will be more than enough to satisfy avian appetites.

JUNEBERRY MUFFINS

This recipe works equally well with fresh, frozen or dried Juneberries. It is also OK to substitute other fruit such as blueberries, raspberries or cranberries in this recipe. The flavor and texture of the muffins will differ somewhat depending on the type of berries you use, but the results are likely to be just as tasty.

INGREDIENTS:

    1 cup rolled oats
    1 cup buttermilk or sour milk (to make sour
    milk, mix 1 cup whole milk with
    1 tablespoon lemon juice or vinegar.)
    1 cup flour
    1 tsp baking powder
    1/2 tsp baking soda
    1/2 tsp salt

Juneberry Muffins

3/4 cup brown sugar, lightly packed (OK to substitute maple sugar)

1 egg, beaten

1/4 cup butter, melted

1 to 1 1/2 cups Juneberries (fresh, frozen or dried – if using dried berries soak in hot fruit juice until softened; frozen fruit need not be completely thawed before using)

PREPARATION:

Combine oats and milk in a small bowl and let stand to allow the oats to soften. Preheat the oven to 400° F. Grease the muffin tins. Combine flour, baking powder, baking soda, salt and brown sugar, and stir well. Mix together the beaten egg and melted butter; combine with oat/milk mixture and mix well. Add oat mixture all at once to the dry ingredients and stir just until all ingredients are moistened (do not overmix). Fold in the Juneberries. Fill muffin tins 3/4 full. Bake for 17-22 minutes until muffin tops turn golden brown.

Makes one dozen muffins.

WILD FRUIT AND NUT GRANOLA

INGREDIENTS:

4 cups oats

1 1/4 cups light or dark brown sugar (OK to substitute Succanat or Maple Sugar)

1/2 tsp. salt

1 cup Shagbark Hickory nuts (see Chapter 11) and/or Black Walnuts (*Juglans nigra*), Butternuts (*Juglans cinerea*) or Hazelnuts (*Corylus spp.*)

1 cup dried Juneberries

1/2 cup shredded coconut (optional)

1/2 cup wheat germ (optional)

1/2 cup peanut or similar-flavored oil

PREPARATION:

Mix all the dry ingredients together in a bowl (except the Juneberries). Add the oil to the mixture and mix thoroughly. Pour the mixture into a 9" by 13" by 2" or larger baking pan and bake at 325° F for 45 minutes, taking care to stir the mixture in the pan every 15 minutes or so to prevent the bottom layer from sticking to the pan. Remove from oven and stir in the dried Juneberries. Once cooled, store in an airtight canister or similar container.

CHAPTER TEN

STAGHORN SUMAC: "RHUS" JUICE, ANYONE?

Mention the name "Sumac" and many people immediately think of the dreaded Poison Sumac (*Toxicodendron vernix*), which reputedly causes even worse skin irritation and blistering than its close relative, Poison Ivy (*Toxicodendron radicans*). Most Sumac species are perfectly harmless — and tasty besides — and are easily distinguishable from Poison Sumac. Poison Sumac has loose, drooping clusters of greenish-white berries that closely resemble those of Poison Ivy, while all other species of Sumac native to Essex County (Staghorn Sumac (*Rhus typhina*), Smooth Sumac (*Rhus glabra*) and Winged Sumac (*Rhus copallinum*)) bear tight, upright clusters of red berries. Furthermore, Poison Sumac is relatively uncommon and isn't usually found outside of wooded swamps, whereas the other Sumac species prefer open, drier ground.

The most commonly encountered Sumac in Essex County, Staghorn Sumac is a large shrub (10 to 12 feet tall) which bears compound leaves with 11-31 pointed leaflets 2-4" long (in contrast, Poison Sumac's leaflets are more egg-shaped and only about an inch or two long). The "staghorn" appellation refers to the fuzzy appearance and feel of the twigs, which is similar to the velvety covering on young deer antlers. Although it is a native species that was once used extensively by Native Americans, Staghorn Sumac goes unappreciated by many as it tends to grow in neglected and highly disturbed landscapes such as abandoned buildings, old fields and vacant lots. To unbiased eyes, however, it is quite attractive, especially in the fall when its leaves turn bright scarlet. Europeans must agree, since they have imported Staghorn Sumac to grow as an ornamental shrub.

The name "Sumac" is derived from the Arabic word for red. The crushed fruits of a Sumac native to the Middle East, *Rhus coriaria*, are used extensively in the cuisine of that region. The barks of several Sumacs have been used as a source of tannic acid for curing leather, which explains why the name "Sumac" has been corrupted to "Shoemake" in some localities. All of the aforementioned plants in the Rhus genus, along with mango and cashew, are members of the Anacardiaceae or Cashew Family. That helps to explain why some people eat raw cashews to try to develop an immunity to Poison Ivy, and why some people get dermatitis from handling raw mangoes.

The most well-known edible portion of Staghorn and all the other edible Sumac species is an acid coating on the outside of the berries consisting of malic acid (the substance that makes apples tart), ascorbic acid (Vitamin C) and tannic acid (one of the flavoring ingredients in tea). Sumacs have both male and female flowers (borne on the same or separate plants), but you will only find berries on the female ones. Staghorn Sumac's yellow-green female flowers bloom in early-to-mid summer, and are followed about a month later by fuzzy red berries in tight, upright, clusters ranging from 3-8 inches in length.

The berries are typically at their best in the latter half of August, but you should be able to locate some flavorful berry clusters weeks or perhaps even months later. Just don't harvest Sumac berries after a big rainstorm, as the rain will wash the acid off (it usually comes back a few days later, although eventually it will wash off for good). To determine whether the berries are ready to be harvested, follow this simple test: lick your index finger, jam it into the center of a berry cluster, wiggle it around a bit and lick your finger again. If you get a strong, pleasing, tart flavor, the berries are good to use. All of the other berry clusters on that same Sumac bush are likely to be at or near the same degree of ripeness.

Harvested Staghorn Sumac berry clusters.

To harvest, just snap the berry clusters off their weak stems. An excellent use for Sumac berries is to make "Sumacade"— some people call this "Indian Lemonade" or "Rhus juice" (after its botanical name). Place the berries into a water-filled container (cold or room-temperature water is best, as very hot water tends to leach too much bitter tannic acid from the berry clusters and ruin the flavor). You will need a dozen or so berry clusters to flavor about a gallon of water. Use your hands to knead and break the berry clusters apart in the water (this gets the flavor off the hairs on the berries and into the water). Then use your hands again to remove the spent berries, squeezing them briefly to release any flavored liquid into the container. Pour the remaining liquid through a sieve lined with a cloth or paper towel to remove any residual berries or other material. The whole process takes only about five minutes.

The liquid will be quite tart, pinkish-orange in color, and could easily pass for unsweetened Pink Lemonade. The tradition of making and drinking Sumacade goes back at least to Colonial times; in fact, it is rumored that Pink Lemonade was invented to mimic the pink color of Sumacade, which people were accustomed to drinking before Lemonade became widely available. Sweeten to taste and serve as a hot or cold beverage. This liquid can also be used as an ingredient in jelly or jam, especially that made with low-acid fruit like Elderberries (see Part Four), which ripen at about the same time. Simply simmer the fruit in Sumacade instead of water, and then proceed with your recipe. Ripe Sumac berry clusters can also be dried for later use.

As Sumacade requires no cooking or fancy preparation equipment, it is one of the easiest wild drinks to make on a camping trip or other outing. I was able to demonstrate this a few years ago while canoeing with some colleagues along the Merrimack River in New Hampshire. I had agreed to stay behind with the boats at the "put-in" point in Franklin while the others shuttled some vehicles to our "take-out" point in Concord. While waiting and looking for something to occupy my time, I noticed a clump of Sumac bushes a short distance away. I gathered a bucketful of ripe fruit clusters, smooshed the clusters in some water, strained it with a clean T-shirt I happened to have on hand, and had the Sumacade ready by the time the others returned.

Fellow forager Sam Thayer from northern Wisconsin (see Bibliography) offers another way to eat Sumac. In mid-spring, the tender new green stems at the growing tips of Sumac branches can be peeled and eaten. The peeled raw stalks are delightfully crisp, juicy and tart, and are great for snacking on the spot or added to a salad. You will have the best luck finding these young stems on the edge of a field or roadside where young plants are resprouting vigorously after having been mowed down. Feel your way down the new stem until it gets stiff and snap it off, peel and eat. (A bit of milky sap may come off as you do this, but it won't affect the flavor.)

One last note of interest: Sumac twigs can be used for tapping Maples and other trees for sap if you run out of metal spiles. Find a section of stem that is about 1/2" in diameter and cut into 3 1/2" lengths. Poke the soft orange pith out of the center of each stem section using a length of metal coat hanger. Then gently tap this hollowed-out stem into the hole you drilled in the tree. You can even cut a small notch at the end of the stem to help hang your sap bucket.

CHAPTER ELEVEN

SHAGBARK HICKORY: FALL FORAGING FUN FOR FRIENDS AND FAMILIES

Shagbark Hickory

Shagbark Hickory (*Carya ovata*) trees are a familiar sight along rural roads and field edges over much of New England as well as further south and west, where they are known as Shellbark Hickories. Their tell-tale bark makes them recognizable year-round. Although other trees (such as Silver Maple (*Acer saccharinum*)) have shaggy bark, none are as dramatically so as Shagbark Hickory. The bark typically pulls away from the trunk in vertical strips over a foot long. Shagbark Hickory's compound leaves are composed of five leaflets, the two inner ones noticeably smaller than the outer three. The trees are typically over 60 feet tall, with trunks a foot or more in diameter. Several other species of smoother-barked Hickories (such as the Pignut, (*Carya glabra*)) can be found in Massachusetts, but their edible nuts tend to be smaller and less tasty than that of the Shagbark. In addition, other Hickory tree species tend to be less numerous in this region and not as conspicuous as Shagbark Hickory.

Shagbark Hickory nuts typically ripen in Essex County over a period of several weeks toward the end of September and into October. The quantity and quality of Hickory nuts can vary considerably from tree to tree and from year to year. Look for trees in sunny spots at the edges of fields or along country roads, as these will tend to bear more and bigger nuts than Hickories shaded by other trees. (If there is a friendly neighborhood dog nearby to scare off the squirrels, so much the better.) One of the most enjoyable ways to find fallen hickory nuts along the edge of the road and adjacent fields is while bicycling through the countryside. Underneath my favorite Shagbark Hickory tree (which happens to be growing along the edge of a farm field in Boxford), I typically find and gather several hundred nuts at a time, and can return to the same spot a week or so later to gather those that have ripened in the interim.

Shagbark Hickory nut meats are enclosed in a smooth, light-tan shell about an inch long that is itself covered by a spherical, shiny-green, four-part husk about two inches in diameter. The nuts usually fall off the tree when they are ripe, so there is no need to pick them off the tree beforehand. The four-parted husk typically splits away from the shell (or is easily pulled off by hand) after the nuts have hit the ground. Occasionally, however, windstorms or squirrels will knock the nuts down before they are fully ripe, and the green husk will be impossible to pry off the shell. In that case, allow the nuts to ripen in their husks by storing them for several weeks in a cool, dry place, such as a garage (make sure that they don't get moldy). Once they are ripe, remove the husks (which may have turned black in the interim). The nuts will keep very well in their shells and should not go bad even after a year or more in storage.

Although considerably thicker than those of their southern relative, the pecan, Shagbark Hickory nut shells can still be cracked open by a sturdy conventional nutcracker. A hammer is also more than adequate, and if you hit the shells at just the right angle, you can extract the nut meat in large pieces (sometimes entire halves) with a minimum of picking. Once you shell the nuts, you should refrigerate or freeze those you don't use or eat within a few days.

After shelling a nut or two and tasting them, you will discover that Shagbark Hickory nuts are delicious and well worth the time spent gathering and shelling them. Their flavor resembles store-bought walnuts that have been lightly sprinkled with maple syrup. They are quite good eaten raw right out of the shell, but are

even better lightly toasted or incorporated into baked goods, like Thumbprint Cookies (see recipe in Chapter Fourteen). Indeed, Hickory nuts' fine flavor makes them a superior substitute for walnuts or pecans in almost any recipe

Hickory nuts and husk

that calls for them. Maple-Hickory Nut Pie (see recipe below) is guaranteed to be a hit with guests as its flavor is richer and less cloying than pecan pie.

Hickory nuts were a very popular food of Northeastern Indian tribes. 17th-century European botanists observed them crushing the shells with stones, and then putting everything (nut meats, shells and all) into mortars, where they would be mixed and pounded with water and then boiled to produce a milky soup- or gruel-like substance which they called "pocohickora" (hence the derivation of the word "Hickory").

Hickories were also greatly appreciated by farm families and other rural folk, who gathered the ripe nuts by the bushel for their own use and for sale in produce markets, where they were a common sight as recently as the 1940s. Since that time, however, our increasingly fast-paced lifestyle seems to have drawn most people toward the convenience of purchasing store-bought, pre-shelled, cultivated nuts such as pecans and walnuts, and the long tradition of gathering wild nuts has largely been lost. Yet, it is hard to imagine a better antidote to the stresses of modern life than spending a splendid fall afternoon in the countryside on a nutting expedition with family or friends. It is but a short leap (literally as well as figuratively) from a "pick your own" apple orchard to gathering nuts at a nearby Hickory tree. Shelling the nuts afterward offers similar rewards, as it makes for a relaxing cold-weather indoor activity, accompanied by a crackling fire, your favorite music or the like. It has a kind of meditative quality to it, like knitting, and with a similar satisfaction of accomplishment once you finish.

One final note: it is allegedly possible to tap Hickory trees in a similar manner to that used on Maple trees and boil down the sap into a sweet syrup, but I have never tried it myself and don't know anyone else who has. (There is a Shagbark Hickory syrup commercially available, but it is made by boiling the bark in sugar syrup and results in an unpleasant-tasting product that to me smells and tastes like water from a Vicks Vaporizer. I'll stick to maple syrup, thank you.)

Maple Hickory-Nut Pie

Pie Crust Ingredients:

> 1 cup flour
> 1/2 tsp salt
> 1/8 cup (2 Tbsp) cold milk
> 1/4 cup vegetable (canola, safflower, corn or soybean) oil

Preparation:

Sift together flour and salt into a bowl. Pour milk and vegetable oil into a measuring cup, but do not stir. Add this liquid to the flour and mix well with a fork. Dampen a table top or

Maple Hickory nut pie

counter with a sponge and smooth a 12-inch square of wax paper on the dampened area. Slightly flatten the dough ball in the center of the wax paper and then cover with another piece of wax paper the same size as the first. Roll the dough between the pieces of wax paper until it reaches the edges and it will be just the right thickness and size for a 9" to 10" diameter pie. Peel off the top paper, turn the dough sheet over into the pie pan, then carefully remove the remaining piece of waxed paper from the top.

Filling Ingredients:

> 3 eggs
> 7/8 cup maple sugar
> 1/2 tsp salt
> 1 cup light corn syrup
> 1/3 cup melted butter
> 1 1/2 to 2 cups Hickory Nuts (no need to chop; large pieces are good for this recipe)

Preparation:

Preheat oven to 350°. Beat the eggs slightly, then add maple sugar, salt, corn syrup and melted butter and beat thoroughly. Stir in the Hickory Nuts, then pour into the unbaked pastry shell. Bake for 50-55 minutes; cool before serving.

Chapter Twelve

Autumn Olive: Not just for the Birds.

Autumn Olive (*Elaeagnus umbellata*) is a spreading shrub about eight feet in height, with silvery-green pointed leaves about two inches long. The shrubs are loaded with small, four-petalled, fragrant yellow flowers that bloom in mid-May. In spite of its name, Autumn Olive is more closely related to (and bears a closer resemblance to) Honeysuckle than to true olives. Russian Olive (*Elaeagnus angustifolia*), which has edible fruit inferior to that of the Autumn Olive, is also a close relative. (Some people mistakenly refer to Autumn Olive as Russian Olive; if the fruit is red it's Autumn Olive.)

Not many people are familiar with Autumn Olive, and for good reason: the plant is a relative newcomer to Essex County. But it has arrived with a vengeance, thanks in large part to the Massachusetts Highway Department, which planted hundreds of plants as ornamentals around highway interchanges for Interstate 95. One needn't risk one's life dodging traffic to pick the fruit, however, as the plant has made itself exceedingly at home throughout the county and elsewhere in the state, primarily in disturbed old field habitat and gravel pits, where its ability to fix nitrogen allows it to thrive in poor topsoil.

Ecological botanists have raised the alarm about the threat this alien invader poses to our landscape. Autumn Olive (along with Japanese Knotweed) was featured in the "Rogues Gallery" of invasive species put out by the New England Wild Flower Society, a botanical equivalent of the FBI's "10 Most Wanted" list. This ignominious status seems somewhat unfair to a plant that was until recently welcomed into our region for its beauty, hardiness and value as bird food (indeed, it has been planted for that very purpose at Audubon sanctuaries). Of those relatively few people who are familiar with Autumn Olive, even fewer know that it is edible by humans and can in fact be quite tasty.

The edible part of Autumn Olive, the ripe fruit, is available over a relatively long period from early October until well into November and occasionally even December, thus providing a good fruit-picking opportunity when nearly everything else is gone. The berries, which are high in Vitamin C, are about the size of large peas and are red with silvery-white dots. Autumn Olive fruit is a joy to pick, as the fruit-bearing branches are usually loaded with hundreds of fruit. It takes no time at all to harvest a gallon or more berries as one stripping motion with your hands is enough to send dozens of berries into your bag or basket. However, you should taste a fruit from each shrub before harvesting. Autumn Olive flavor can vary considerably from shrub to shrub, and some are too astringent.

When you find the right combination of sweetness and tartness, all the fruit on that particular shrub should have the same great flavor, which is similar to green Thompson seedless grapes. Since Autumn Olive fruit has seeds, however (which are not disagreeable when eaten raw), the first prerequisite to using it in recipes is to separate the pulp from the seeds. To do this, first put the fruit in a large pot with just enough water to keep the fruit from scorching (approximately 1/8th inch deep). Simmer for about 1/2 hour, stirring occasionally, until the fruit has softened. Then run everything through a food mill to separate the seeds from the pulp. If you

Ellen Vliet Cohen sniffing Autumn Olive blooms on Misery Island in Salem.

don't have a food mill, you can mash up the softened fruit in the pot with a potato masher, then pour the contents out into a sieve and stir briskly. The sieve holds back the seeds and lets the fruit pulp go through. At this point you will have a frothy, mauve-colored purée, which can serve as raw material for many different preparations.

A delicious and simple recipe made from Autumn Olive purée is fruit leather (similar to the fruit roll-ups that children are so fond of). I often serve Autumn Olive Fruit Leather to my students at the beginning of my classes while waiting for everyone to arrive, and nearly everybody raves about its distinctive sweet and tart flavor. Though it is easiest to make it with a food dehydrator, it is possible to do it with cookie trays (with rims) in your oven. I highly recommend getting a food dehydrator, as they are great for processing many conventional as well as wild foods, and are especially handy for drying wild mushrooms. (I am very satisfied with the model I use, a cylindrical type with stackable trays, which is available for about $60 at many hardware and kitchen stores. Don't forget to purchase the accessory fruit roll sheet if you want to make fruit leather.) To make fruit leather, simply pour the Autumn Olive purée onto the liquid-holding trays and run the dehydrator it until the purée dries to the right consistency (about 21 hours). The resulting fruit leather is made from 100% pure organic Autumn Olive fruit pulp; nothing else (sugar, lemon juice, etc.) is added. This same purée also makes good raw material for ice cream or sorbet, and would probably work well in chiffon pie recipes.

One last noteworthy item about this plant: it is an excellent source of lycopene, a powerful antioxidant found in some reddish fruits that may help prevent prostate cancer and other forms of cancer, heart disease and other serious diseases. A recent study conducted by the U.S. Department of Agriculture found that lycopene levels in raw Autumn Olive fruit are up to 18 times higher than tomatoes. If, like tomatoes, cooking the fruit makes the lycopene more available for absorption by the human body, products made from the simmered and pureed Autumn Olive fruit (like the fruit leather) should be an even richer source of this health-promoting substance.

CHAPTER THIRTEEN

JERUSALEM ARTICHOKE - AN "OFF-SEASON" FORAGING OPPORTUNITY

The common name Jerusalem Artichoke (*Helianthus tuberosus*) is more than a little misleading, as the plant is neither from Jerusalem, nor is it an artichoke. "Jerusalem" is a corruption of the Spanish word "girasole," which means sunflower; and "artichoke" is thought to refer to the artichoke-like flavor of the tubers. The plant is a close relative of the Sunflower and a distant cousin of the Artichoke. They are all in the Asteraceae or Composite Family, a large botanical family that has many edible wild plants, including Ox-eye Daisy (*Chrysanthemum leucanthemum*), Dandelion (*Taraxacum officinale*), Burdock (*Arctium spp.*) and Chicory (*Cichorium intybus*), all of which are described in Part Four.

Like Sunflowers, Jerusalem Artichokes are native to the Central United States, but have been naturalized in New England. Like many of the native species discussed in this book, Jerusalem Artichokes were well-used by Native Americans. It is believed that Jerusalem Artichokes were brought to New England through trade between local and Midwestern tribes. Early French explorers to the New World subsequently introduced the plant to Europe in the 17th Century.

Unlike Groundnut, a number of cultivated forms of Jerusalem Artichoke have been successfully developed. You may see their tubers for sale in your supermarket's specialty produce section (where they are often referred to as "sun chokes"). Jerusalem Artichoke also occasionally shows up as an ingredient in some specialty processed food items like pasta. The form that starch takes in Jerusalem Artichoke tubers (inulin) apparently is good for diabetic diets.

Assuming that you are looking for a more "earthy" way to get Jerusalem Artichoke tubers than buying pasta at your grocery store, here are some helpful hints. Jerusalem Artichoke is, unfortunately, among the harder-to-recognize edible wild plants. Although the plant usually produces small, Sunflower-like flowers that bloom in mid- to late summer, Jerusalem

Jerusalem Artichoke flowers in bloom

Artichoke is so successful at propagating itself through its tubers that it sometimes doesn't bother to bloom at all.

Without the flowers, Jerusalem Artichoke could easily be mistaken for its close cousin, Sunflower, as its leaves and stalks are quite similar in size and appearance. One difference is that the rough, sandpaper-like Jerusalem Artichoke leaves are narrower than Sunflower leaves. Another important distinguishing characteristic is that Jerusalem Artichoke almost invariably grows in patches five or more feet in diameter, which are typically found in partial shade on the edges of fields, roads, and similar habitats. Sunflowers typically don't grow in patches.

Another challenge presented by Jerusalem Artichoke is that, unlike Groundnut, the tubers are available for harvesting only during the colder months, when the above-ground foliage is least noticeable. This is another good illustration of why it's worth noting the location of edible plants at their most visible stage so you can find them later at harvest time.

Jerusalem Artichoke tubers are in season from late October to March, and can be harvested any

Jerusalem Artichoke tubers

time the ground isn't frozen. The tubers lie a couple of inches below the surface, and usually are set out radially, attached to thin rootlets a short distance from each stalk. They range in size and shape from a gumball to a fat knobby cigar, and their skin is usually beige or mauve in color. If you find a good-sized patch in rich soil you can collect a bucketful of tubers in less than an hour. They will keep for a few weeks in the refrigerator, or can be frozen.

If the ground is soft, dig the tubers out by hand or with a trowel, shovel or pitchfork. Don't be too concerned about wiping out a Jerusalem Artichoke patch through overharvesting — it is unlikely that you will find all of the tubers, and those that elude your search will sprout up in the spring and eventually produce a new crop. In fact, some Jerusalem Artichoke patches grow too thick for their own good and can actually benefit from being thinned. Nevertheless, I typically replace the smallest tubers I dig up back into the hole I dug them from to help ensure a sustainable harvest.

Jerusalem Artichoke tubers can be peeled and eaten raw in salads (although some people find the raw tubers are gas producing); their crunchy texture is reminiscent of water chestnuts. This quality also makes them excellent pickle material. The tubers are also good boiled and mashed or baked *au gratin* in a casserole. They make a good substitute for potatoes in many dishes, such as Cattail Chowder (see Cattail chowder recipe in Chapter Six) or Vichyssoise. Another great way of cooking Jerusalem Artichoke tubers is simply to place them in the pan around a leg of lamb or other meat that will roast in the oven.

You can also make your own fresh homemade pasta with Jerusalem Arichokes. This has to be done in several steps, and is made considerably easier if you have the appropriate equipment. Here's a rather high-tech way to do it. First, cover the bottom of a baking dish with a couple dozen whole raw tubers, and bake at 350° until soft (about 20-30 minutes). After removing them from the oven and waiting until they are cool enough to handle, slice the tubers into rounds about 1/8 inch thick, and then place the slices on the trays of a food dehydrator. (If you prefer, you can skip the baking step and dehydrate raw tuber slices, but I have found that pasta made from raw tubers causes more gas than if they are baked first.) After the slices have been thoroughly dried (this typically takes several hours), put them into a food processor and pulverize until at least a portion is ground to the consistency of flour. (The larger pieces can be sifted out and stored in a glass jar in the cupboard for regrinding or other uses). Next, measure out about one part Jerusalem Artichoke flour to three or so parts semolina flour and place into the bowl of an automatic pasta maker. Add about half of whatever liquid a typical pasta recipe calls for to get the dough to extrude properly from the pasta maker.

Once the pasta is made: if you don't cook it up right away, you can keep it in the refrigerator for a day or so, or store it in the freezer for later use. Store-bought Jerusalem Artichoke or most other flavored noodles (such as spinach or tomato) can hardly be distinguished from the unflavored kind once you boil them. In contrast, homemade pasta made from Jerusalem Artichoke retains its strong and distinctive flavor, even though they may only make up a small proportion of the dough.

CHAPTER FOURTEEN

BARBERRY:
A GREAT REMEDY
FOR CABIN FEVER

Before extolling the culinary virtues of the Common, or European, Barberry (*Berberis vulgaris*), it is important first to distinguish it from the nefarious Japanese Barberry (*Berberis thunbergii*), a plant at or near the top of the invasive species blacklists.

Japanese Barberry has become a serious pest in southern New England, especially in old fields, pastures and early successional woodlands. It is of particular concern in the Berkshires, where it invades and degrades rich woodland habitats relied upon by spring ephemeral wildflowers and rare plant species. Japanese Barberry is easy to distinguish from European Barberry once you know what to look for. Japanese Barberry rarely gets over 3-4 feet tall. It has small, untoothed leaves and a single spine beneath each cluster of leaves. Its orange-red berries are borne singly on the underside of the twigs. In contrast, European Barberry typically grows 6-8 feet tall, has toothed leaves and two-or three-branched spines beneath each cluster of leaves. Its egg-shaped, centimeter-long, deep red berries hang in drooping clusters of a dozen or so and are much juicier and tastier than Japanese Barberries, which tend to be dry and bitter. One way to remember which is which is that Japan is just one country (i.e., singly-borne berries) whereas Europe is many countries (i.e. berries borne in a cluster). (To complicate matters, however, these two species occasionally hybridize and the resulting plant bears some resemblance to both.)

In the 18th century, *B. vulgaris* (meaning "common" in Latin) was indeed more common in these parts than Japanese Barberry, which didn't arrive in New England until the late 1800s (after the other species got its "vulgaris" botanical name). Japanese Barberry was (and unfortunately still sometimes is) extensively planted as a hedge and valued for its colorful fall foliage. The so-called Common Barberry is now a misnomer, as it is decidedly less common than its more heavily planted and invasive cousin. Japanese Barberry is actually the more "vulgar" of the two, at least from an ecological and edibility perspective. (A significant down side to Common Barberry, however, is that it hosts a wheat rust fungus, and thus many wheat-producing states prohibit it from being planted.)

Although too seedy and tart to be good as a raw fruit, European Barberries have a delicious flavor quite similar (but superior to) cranberries. Yet, because they are not as readily available as cranberries, relatively few people use them today. This was not always the case. Barberries were well-known and appreciated by Massachusetts households of the Colonial and subsequent periods. An article appearing in the periodical New England Farmer in the early 1800s stated, "Barberry jelly, ruby clear, is the finest table jelly to serve with venison and other high-flavored roasts, and epicures will have no other when they have once tried it."

Barberry blossoms

New England housewives often put Barberries into the jars of other preserved fruits to add a tart flavor. Henry David Thoreau took note of the spirited competition over Barberries in his native Concord; he observed the townspeople going out to pick them as early as mid-September (before they were fully ripe) to gather the fruit first. Merritt Lyndon Fernald, a renowned professor of botany at Harvard during the first half of this century, wrote (in 1942), "In the regions where it abounds, the Barberry has always been a favorite fruit for spiced preserves, jellies and other similar preparations."

Barberry plants can still be found growing alongside 18th and 19th century farmhouses and rural roads. A good time to locate Barberry bushes is in May, when the bushes are covered with clusters of yellow blossoms and a heavy (and somewhat unpleasant) scent. The blossoms are followed by deep red berries that ripen in the fall and typically persist on the bushes into the winter, and occasionally into the following spring. (One year I made Barberry Jelly in May from the previous season's berries still clinging to plants that had already begun to flower.) One doesn't ordinarily think of berry-picking while on a mid-winter outing, but Barberries can provide that fun foraging opportunity.

The berries are ripe and at their juiciest in mid-autumn. If you are able to extract enough juice from the berries for a batch of jelly without adding water (by, e.g., heating them in a crock and squeezing the juice out of the softened berries), you will find that they contain enough pectin to make jelly. If, however, you wait to gather them until the shriveled (but still highly flavored) fruit looks like little red raisins, you will need to simmer them in a little water first for a half hour or so. Remove the seeds (which resemble the small pegs once used in shoemaking) by pouring the resulting product through a sieve, and combine with crabapple juice or use commercial pectin to get it to jell. With an equal bulk of sugar to juice, Barberry makes a very tart, distinctly flavored jelly that works particularly well in Thumbprint Cookies (see below).

Barberry juice adds a red color and tart flavor to apple juice, apple sauce and stewed Japanese Knotweed stalks.

Several years ago, I was attempting to make a batch of Barberry jelly and found that the liquid didn't jell after it cooled. As I didn't have the time or the patience at that point to reheat the liquid, add more pectin or juice and try again (a method that has worked on other occasions), I poured the liquid into a plastic container, stuck it in the back of the fridge and soon forgot all about it. Three months later, when I rediscovered it, it had scum on the top, sediment on the bottom and was quite lethal-looking. I was about to pitch it when I decided, just for the sake of scientific curiosity, to stick a spoon in it and see what happened. I took one sip and had to laugh because it turned out to be the best wine I have ever tasted: very fruity, with a delightfully smooth finish. Unfortunately, as this was a complete accident, I can't provide you with an exact recipe; all I can tell you is that Barberries make great wine.

A few final words about Barberry: Both the red berries and the bright yellow wood of Barberries are used to dye fabric and other articles. The bark of Barberry stems and roots is considered by herbalists to be one of the best remedies for correcting liver function and promoting the flow of bile. A recent Chinese study showed that berberine, the primary active medicinal compound in *Berberis* species, is as effective as statins in lowering "bad" (LDL) cholesterol. Lastly, two other wild edible members of the Barberry family (*Berberidaceae*), Oregon Grape (*Mahonia aquifolium*) and May Apple (*Podophyllum peltatum*), can occasionally be found in Massachusetts (although probably not in anything other than a horticultural setting in Essex County).

THUMBPRINT COOKIES

INGREDIENTS:

1/2 cup soft shortening (OK to substitute 1/2 cup butter or margarine)
1/4 cup light brown sugar
1 large egg, separated
1/2 teaspoon vanilla extract
1 cup flour
1 pinch salt
1 cup or more Hickory Nuts, finely chopped (Black Walnuts or store-bought walnuts can be substituted if necessary)
1/3 cup sparkling jelly (Barberry or Crabapple Jelly work particularly well)

Thumbprint cookies

PREPARATION:

Mix thoroughly together shortening, brown sugar, egg yolk and vanilla extract; add flour and salt gradually to the mixture. Mix the dough together until dry spots disappear. Preheat oven to 375º F. Wet hands and roll dough into balls 1 inch in diameter. Dip each ball into slightly beaten eggwhite, then roll each ball into chopped hickory nuts. Place about 1 inch apart on ungreased cookie sheet. Cook 5 minutes at 375º. Remove from oven and press thumb gently into the center of each cookie to make a depression; return cookies to the oven and bake for 8 minutes more. Remove from the oven; check to make sure depressions are still there; if not, press thumb in again. Cool, then fill the depressions with jelly.

Makes about 15 cookies.

PART FOUR

TASTY TIDBITS

ABOUT MORE WILD EDIBLES

Wild Strawberries

Before ending this book, I wanted to share with you some interesting tidbits about a number of my other foraging favorites. The plants I include in this last section range from those you already know well (Like Daisy and Dandelion) to plants you may have never even heard of (like Calamus and Carrion Flower). Like the 14 species featured in Part Three, all of the following plants are fine-flavored, grow in Essex County (and, in most cases, far beyond), and are readily distinguishable from poisonous look-alikes. Because many plants described in this section have long and/or multiple periods of availability, I chose to present them alphabetically by common name. Here they are:

BEACH PEAS (*Lathyrus maritimus*) Beach Peas have a long season of availability and can usually be found at an edible stage all summer long. Look for the plants just above the "wrack" (extreme high tide) line, especially in sandy areas. I prefer to harvest pods with bright green, tender peas inside. These tender shelled peas can be used any way you'd use garden peas. Beach Pea tendrils (the young growing tips of the plants) can also be steamed and eaten in a similar manner to conventional pea tendrils. [Note: while, during times of famine, some people primarily relying upon members of the *Lathyrus* genus for food have developed a debilitating neurological condition called lathyrism, this is not considered a concern for people who eat beach peas as part of a normally diverse diet.]

BEACH PLUMS (*Prunus maritima*) Beach Plums can be found along much of Essex County's extensive coastline, most notably on Plum Island. Like Juneberries, Beach Plum bushes are most easily located in spring when the plants are in bloom. However, Beach Plums ripen much later, from August into mid-September. Their size and flavor varies considerably, but at their best, Beach Plums are about 3/4 inch in diameter, with an appealing flavor and texture that is scarcely distinguishable from cultivated plums. Often the fruit has a slight bitterness to it, which is not at all a disadvantage when the fruit is used for making jam or jelly.

BURDOCK (*Arctium spp.*) Burdock is the plant that produces those round burrs that get stuck to your socks in the fall. (The fellow who invented Velcro™, George de Mestral from Switzerland, got the idea from those burrs.) Burdock is quite nutritious, and is highly valued in Asian and macrobiotic cuisine. The plants are readily available in vacant lots, and along the edges of farm and athletic fields and similar habitats. Burdocks are a "biennial" species, which means they have a two-year life cycle. Burdock roots are best for harvesting between the middle of the plants' first growing season to the beginning of the second growing season (i.e., from July of the first year to April of the second year). For those who would rather avoid strenuous digging, an equally edible portion of the Burdock plant is the developing flower stalk, which appears during the second growing season. Harvest the stalk when it is about 1-2 feet high and still growing (much before the flowers show up); Burdocks are usually at this stage in Essex County the first two weeks of June. When you get the bloom stalks home, peel or cut off the outer rind (which tends to be stringy and bitter). Then, chop the peeled bloom stalks into rounds about 1/3 inch thick and boil until tender (about five minutes). Boiled Burdock roots or flower stalks have an artichoke-like flavor (the plants are cousins) and can be eaten as is or substituted for artichoke hearts in many recipes. Last but not least, Burdock petioles (leaf stalks) gathered in the spring can be boiled until tender, dipped into beaten eggs, rolled in seasoned bread crumbs, shaped into patties, and fried in olive oil until golden.

CALAMUS (*Acorus calamus*) Calamus typically grows in patches 20-50 feet in diameter in wet grassy meadows, along the shallow margins of rivers, or in damp spots in cow pastures. Calamus has a similar appearance to Cattails, although Calamus only grows about half as tall and its leaves are more yellow in color. Calamus is also referred to as Sweet Flag, and is similar in appearance and habitat preference to the poisonous Blue Flag (*Iris versicolor*). The plants are easy to distinguish when in bloom in that the showy Blue Flag Iris flowers are violet-blue and yellow in color and grow on a stalk at the top of the plant, whereas Sweet Flag flowers are the same color as the leaves and stick out at an angle like a skinny thumb from the side of the leaf clusters. Another distinguishing characteristic of Calamus is that the whole plant exudes a strong, ginger-like spicy flavor, which is most noticeable in the root. In earlier times, it was a common custom to chew on a bit of candied Calamus root as an after-dinner sweet and digestive aid. My favorite part of the Calamus plant is the heart – the tender, yellowish-white inner leaves in the center of each growing plant. These taste similar to the root but are much milder and can be used raw to add a spicy zing to salads. The hearts are available in the spring and into the early summer.

CARRION FLOWER (*Smilax herbacea*) Look for Carrion Flower along the sunny edges of wooded swamps; the shoots are at the harvestable stage during the latter half of May. Carrion Flower is aptly named in that the foul odor emanating from its greenish, spherical flower clusters is reminiscent of a dead animal. When this thornless, tender cousin of Cat Brier (*Smilax rotundifolia*) is in the shoot stage (i.e., before the stinky flowers bloom), it bears a strong resemblance to Asparagus (to which it is also related). Simply break off the top 6-12 inches of the shoot, then cook and eat just like Asparagus.

CATNIP (*Nepeta cataria*) Catnip, like most of its brethren in the Mint Family (Lamiaceae), has square-shaped (four-sided) stems and opposite leaves. Although best known as a cultivated garden plant, it occasionally establishes wild populations along roadsides, pathways and field edges. Catnip has the opposite effect on people as it has on cats: it acts as a mild tranquillizer and sedative. Catnip tea is great for anyone looking to calm down after a stressful day. Tea can be made with either fresh or dried leaves; the number of leaves used depends on how strong you want the flavor to be. I find a couple tablespoons of leaves per mug to be the right amount.

CHICKWEED (*Stellaria media*) Chickweed, an extremely common farm and garden weed, can be harvested in the spring, fall, and even during a mild winter. The plant consists of clumps of prostrate stems with clusters of smooth, small leaves at the joints, typically sporting small white, star-like flowers. If you look carefully, you may see a thin line of hairs running along one side of the stem, which switch to the opposite side at each joint. All aboveground parts of Chickweed are edible both raw and cooked; the raw stems taste like raw corn, and the cooked leaves taste like spinach. Raw Chickweed makes an excellent lettuce or sprout substitute in salads and sandwiches. Harvest by picking the tender, newer, "leafier" portion on the outside of the clumps; leave the "stemmier" center part alone.

CHICORY (*Cichorium intybus*) Chicory, a 2-3 foot tall plant with blue, dandelion-like flowers, is a common sight along roadsides and field edges in summer. The most well-known edible portion of Chicory is the root, which is used as a coffee additive or substitute; the root can be gathered any time for this purpose. Spread the washed roots on a cookie sheet and roast slowly at 250-300° for 2-4 hours, until the roots are brittle and aromatic. Grind the roots in a food processor to the consistency of coffee grounds; then brew these grounds in just the same way you would to make coffee (you'll only need about 1/2 the amount of Chicory grounds as coffee to make the same strength beverage). Chicory coffee tastes remarkably like regular coffee but does not have caffeine in it. Young Chicory leaves are edible in the spring before the hot weather arrives and again in the fall when the cool weather returns. The blue flowers are also edible; they don't have much flavor, but as blue is an unusual food color, it is fun to snip the petals off to decorate salads or other dishes.

CURLED DOCK (*Rumex crispus*) Curled Dock was mentioned in Chapter One as a well-known topical remedy for the sting of Stinging Nettle. It has an even better reputation for its edible and medicinal qualities. When mature, Curled Dock leaves are 9-14 inches long, with a decidedly wavy leaf margin. The younger, unfurled leaves at the center of each Dock plant are the mildest and tastiest. These are available in mid-spring and (to a lesser extent) in the fall. I prefer to blanch Dock leaves briefly (immersing them for 30-60 seconds in boiling water) before using them in soups or other cooked dishes (see Wild Greens Spanikopita recipe). The developing flower stalk can be peeled and eaten raw and has a nice crunchy, juicy quality. The herbalists' name for Curled Dock is Yellow Dock, as the big yellow taproot is used medicinally to — among other things — help the body assimilate iron.

DAME'S ROCKET (*Hesperis matronalis*) Dame's Rocket, a close relative of Mustard, Radish and Arugula, produces a large quantity of edible white and/or purple four-petaled flowers about an inch in diameter. (Many people mistakenly refer to Dame's Rocket as "Phlox" because of its similar flower color, but all Phlox Family flowers have five petals, whereas Dame's Rocket and its fellow members in the Mustard Family have four.) The flowers are available for about a month in May and early June. Their delightful flavor is suggestive of a sweet radish with garlic undertones. They are great eaten on the spot, or brought home to liven up a salad or serve as an attractive and tasty garnish. Placed in a plastic storage bag with a piece of damp paper towel, they'll keep for a week or two in the refrigerator. Don't worry about picking too many, as Dame's Rocket is an invasive species and the ecologists are glad to have your help in keeping it under control.

DANDELIONS (*Taraxacum spp.*) Once people hear that dandelions are edible they often immediately go out to pick and eat a few leaves from their back yard; upon tasting the incredibly bitter flavor, however, they might swear off wild edibles forever. Dandelions are very tasty, but the trick is to harvest them early (in Essex County, the latter half of April and early May), before the flowers emerge. In fact, the unopened flower buds are one of the tastiest parts of the plant. If you locate some large plants (look at the edges of farm and athletic fields), you can often find more than 100 flower buds per plant — enough to supplement a meal for you and your dinner guests. Once you get the buds home, put them in a container of cold water and stir briskly to remove any dirt or grit. Boil a pot of water, then add the Dandelion buds and boil for no more than 60 seconds; they're ready to eat as is, freeze for later use, or incorporate into other dishes such as casseroles, omelets, soups and the like. Their surprisingly delectable flavor is like a cross between corn, spinach, artichokes, and Brussels sprouts.

DAY LILIES (*Hemerocallis spp.*) Day Lilies have been a popular garden plant in Essex County for more than a century. Many readers of this book have probably already eaten Day Lilies, since dried Day Lily flowers are a standard ingredient in such Chinese dishes as Moo Shu and Hot and Sour Soup. Five different parts of Day Lilies are considered edible, however, a small segment of the population (less than 5%) will experience digestive upset when eating Day Lilies (especially uncooked), so it is wise to start with modest amounts to see how well your system can handle them. The first edible segment is the cluster of yellowish-tan starchy tubers that lay underground at the base of each plant. These are edible raw or cooked like a potato (baked, boiled, mashed). Day Lily hearts, the tender inner growth at the center of each developing cluster of leaves, may be eaten raw or used like scallions (which they resemble in flavor). Day Lily flower buds, flowers and wilted flowers are also all edible. Sauté the buds in butter for a few minutes in a frying pan to get a vegetable very similar in character to green beans. The oniony flower petals can be eaten just as is, mixed into a salad or fried in batter. The wilted flowers can be added to soups or stews to add body and flavor. All Day Lilies are edible, regardless of flower color and whether the plants are wild or cultivated.

ELDERBERRY (*Sambucus canadensis*) Elderberry, a relatively common shrub in eastern Massachusetts and beyond, typically inhabits damp meadows. In Essex County, Elderberries are ripe at the tail end of summer and into early fall, when the berries are a very dark purplish-black and their weight makes the clusters hang upside down. You will need to cook or dry the Elderberries to render them safely edible. I find Elderberries to be too strongly aromatic to be used on their own, but very good mixed with blander fruit like apples. Apple-Elderberry sauce or Apple-Elderberry pie is much more interesting than that made with just apples. Elderberries are high in Vitamin C and other vitamins and minerals, and have a reputation for being effective against the flu and other ailments. Elderberry plants bloom in early June in Essex County, and some people like to make a cordial (an alcoholic or non-alcoholic beverage) from the flowers, or cook them up into fritters (but fritters made from Black Locust flowers are much tastier).

EVENING PRIMROSE (*Oenothera biennis*) Evening Primrose can often be found in vacant lots and disturbed ground. Like Burdock (see above), Evening Primrose has a biennial (two-year) life cycle. The first year, Evening Primrose produces a flat rosette (whorl) of leaves and sends food energy down to an ivory-colored (tinged with pink at the top), carrot-like taproot. The second year, the plant uses the energy in that taproot to produce a 3-4 foot tall flower stalk with lemon-yellow colored flowers. At the end of the second season, the plant goes to seed and dies. Evening Primrose roots are best for harvesting during the dormant period between their first and second growing seasons (i.e., from October of the first year to April of the second year). The roots can be used most ways one would use a cooked root vegetable; my favorite way of using them is to grate them up and make "primrose pancakes" in a similar manner as potato pancakes.

Ground Cherry

GROUND CHERRY (*Physalis spp.*) Ground Cherries, also known as husk tomato or strawberry tomato, are in fact a wild edible cousin of the tomato. The plants typically grow along the edges of pastures, meadows and mowed or cultivated fields. Ground Cherries are not common, so it is always a treat to find them. Ground cherries can be easily distinguished from their poisonous look-alikes by the fact that each small (1/3- to 1/2-inch in diameter) fruit is encased in a papery, beige-colored husk. Like tomatoes, Ground Cherry plants don't really start to grow until all danger of frost is past and the warmer weather arrives. The fruits start to form on the plants in mid-summer, but usually don't ripen until the fall. The ripening fruits (still enclosed in their husks) typically fall off the plant and finish ripening on the ground underneath the plant. Ripe Ground Cherries are yellowish in color and look and taste quite similar to a miniature sweet tomato. They are excellent for eating raw on the spot, served in a salad, or cooked up into pies and preserves.

JEWELWEED (*Impatiens capensis*) Jewelweed is an annual, native plant that prefers damp, shady areas and typically grows to about three feet in height. The plant may have gotten its common name from its pretty orange flowers (with distinctive skinny tails), or from the fact that rain droplets beading up on the plant's unwettable leaves sparkle in the sun. The botanical name Impatiens, as well as the plant's other common name Touch-me-not, comes from the plant's ripe seed pods which explode upon the slightest contact, propelling the seeds several feet away. Jewelweed is probably best known as an antidote to Poison Ivy (it can also be used as an antidote to the sting of Stinging

Nettle (see Chapter One). Rub the above-ground portions of the plant on your skin any place you have the Poison Ivy (or Nettle) rash, or on skin you suspect was exposed to Poison Ivy. For a remedy you can keep at home, simply boil up some Jewelweed, pour the liquid from the pot into some ice cube trays, and freeze. Jewelweed is also edible. I recommend eating the ripe seeds, which taste just like walnuts, and are available from mid-summer into the early fall. The seeds are a challenge to gather as they tend to shoot out every which way from the exploding pods. The trick is to have the ripe pod explode in your hand to capture the seeds — brownish-green football-shaped objects about 1/8 inch long. By the way, if you slip off the outer cover on one of those ripe seeds (which is not necessary to eat them), you will discover that the color of the seed itself is a remarkable robins-egg blue.

LAMBS QUARTERS (*Chenopodium album)* Lambs Quarters goes by several names, including Pigweed, Wild Spinach and White Goosefoot (a translation of *Chenopodium album*, its botanical name). Lambs Quarters can be found in gardens and other disturbed fertile soil the world over. You can recognize Lambs Quarters by the goosefoot-shaped leaves and the whitish dust in the center of each growing leaf cluster. All tender above-ground portions of the plant (leaves and stems) are edible and are best when the plant is 3-7 inches high. In Essex County, this typically occurs in late May to early June, but, like other opportunistic weeds, young Lamb's Quarters plants can often be found throughout the growing season. Lamb's Quarters is very mild in flavor and can be eaten raw or cooked. It is an excellent substitute in any recipe that calls for spinach, and it has a higher vitamin content than spinach. It is also possible to collect the poppy seed-like seeds from mature Lamb's Quarters plants in the fall and grind them up into a buckwheat-like flour.

MULBERRY (*Morus rubra*) and (*Morus alba*) Mulberry trees are typically found in or near built-up areas, field edges or in disturbed habitats. Both Red (*Morus rubra*) and White (*Morus alba*) Mulberries grow in Essex County, and often hybridize with each other. The ripe, blackberry-like fruit of both species is edible and (along with Juneberry) is among the first to ripen in the area. The ripe fruit varies considerably in flavor from tree to tree. White Mulberries tend to be sweet without any tartness, as are fully-ripe red mulberries (which turn a purplish-black color when fully ripe — pick them slightly underripe for a tangier flavor). You can eat the fruit on the spot, bring it home and make into pies, preserves or fruit drinks, or dry or freeze for later use. It is also worth noting that young Mulberry leaves (before they fully unfurl) can be steamed for an excellent spinach-like side dish.

OX-EYE DAISY (*Chrysanthemum leucanthemum*) Ox-eye Daisy is the common and familiar flower that has traditionally been used in the "she loves me – she loves me not" petal-picking game. The young leaves and unopened buds of Ox-eye Daisy are the tastiest portion of the plant. These are available in Essex County for several weeks beginning around Mother's Day. Their sweet, succulent and slightly spicy flavor makes them excellent salad material. Ox-eye daisy's poisonous look-alike, Daisy Fleabane, also has white petals with yellow centers, but is very easy to distinguish from Ox-eye Daisy; to play the "she loves me, she loves me not" game with Daisy Fleabane, you'd need a set of tweezers because the individual petals are too narrow to pick by hand. Furthermore, Daisy Fleabane's leaves look quite different from Ox-eye Daisy's and taste horrible.

PARTRIDGEBERRY (*Michella repens*) Partridgeberry plants are a common ground cover in cool, shady woodlands and are often found under pines and hemlocks. The plant's short, prostrate branches bear opposite pairs of small, roundish, dark-green leaves with prominent white midribs. The edible portion of the plant is its bright red, Tic Tac™-sized and shaped berries, which develop in the late summer but often persist until the following spring. Each berry has two little belly-button-like markings instead of just one, like blueberries and other fruit. This is because each Partridgeberry fruit is the product of two flowers that are fused at the base. Although Partridgeberries have virtually no flavor, their bright red color adds color and interest to a salad.

PINEAPPLEWEED (*Matricaria matricariodes*) Pineappleweed, a close cousin of Chamomile, also shares Chamomile's appearance and usage. Pineappleweed is so named because the whole plant — in particular its conical-shaped, petal-less yellow-flowers — smell when crushed just like canned pineapple. Look for Pineappleweed plants in poor, gravelly soil, like that found in vacant lots and along the edges of gravel pathways and roads (but do not harvest from heavily-traveled roadways and other areas you suspect might have accumulated pollutants). The flowers are best for harvesting in Essex County around mid-June. A pleasant-tasting, pineapple-scented tea can be made by steeping a tablespoon or two of the fresh or dried flowers in a mug of hot water for a few minutes.

SHEEP SORREL (*Rumex acetosella*) Sheep Sorrel, an introduced weed from Europe, is typically found in old fields, pastures and similar disturbed habitats. Sheep sorrel is easily recognizable by its distinctive, arrowhead-shaped leaves which are about 1-3 inches long. Sheep Sorrel flowers are reddish-brown in color, and small-to-large patches of the plants are a common sight on highway medians in the spring. The edible portion of the plant — the young leaves — is tastiest when harvested in the spring before the plants bloom, and before the onset of hot weather. Plants that grow in damp spots out of the full sun produce the lushest and most succulent leaves. "Acetosella" means "little vinegar plant" in Latin, and Sheep Sorrel leaves have an appealing juicy, lemony flavor. These leaves make an excellent tart salad ingredient, and can be used in place of its cultivated cousin French or Garden Sorrel (*Rumex acetosa*). The chemical responsible for the sour taste in Sheep Sorrel is oxalic acid, which could hurt your stomach lining and/or inhibit your body's ability to uptake calcium if eaten in huge amounts (e.g., a big salad bowl composed entirely of this plant). Oxalic acid is present in many conventional vegetables like beets, spinach and rhubarb, so as long as you eat these foods in moderation you have no need to worry.

VIOLETS (*Viola sororia*) Although all Violets (*Viola spp.*) edible, over a half dozen are on Massachusetts' "T and E" (Threatened and Endangered) list, so you should confine your harvesting to the Common or Dooryard Violet (*Viola sororia*), also referred to as the "Blue" Violet. True to its name, the Common Violet is by far the most common, and can be found in the same grassy habitat as Dandelions (which also bloom around the same time). Leaf shape is an important identifying characteristic in Violet species. The Common Violet leaves are heart-shaped, with the young, curled-up leaves emerging from the center of the plant. These young leaves, along with the flowers, are edible. The leaves may be eaten raw or cooked and are very high in both Vitamins A and C. The raw flowers can be used to decorate salads or other dishes, or can be candied or made into jelly. Once the plant has finished blooming, however, the leaves become tough and bitter.

WHITE OAK ACORNS (*Quercus alba*) White Oak is the most common of the so-called "soft" oak species, all of which have leaves with rounded lobes (as opposed to the "hard" oak species with pointy lobes —see right-hand leaf in photo). Acorns from White Oak and the other "soft" oak species are lower in tannic acid and therefore less bitter than acorns from the "hard" oak species. Acorn flour lends a delicious and distinctive flavor to muffins, cakes, breads and other baked goods. To make acorn flour, shell the acorns, and (if their bitterness is still too strong for your taste) leach out some of the tannic acid by boiling the shelled nuts for a few minutes in several changes of water. Dry the nut meats by spreading them out on a cookie sheet and sticking them in a warm oven for a few hours, then pulverize them in a food processor until they are the consistency of flour or a fine-grained meal.

WILD GRAPES (*Vitis riparia, Vitis aestivalis* and *Vitis labrusca*) There are three species of Wild Grapes that grow in eastern Massachusetts: the Riverside Grape (*Vitis riparia*), the Summer Grape (*Vitis aestivalis*) and the Fox Grape (*Vitis labrusca*). (As Summer Grapes are similar to Fox Grapes, I lump them together.) Although all three species are edible, one or another is better depending on what you want to eat or make with the plant. Fox/Summer Grapes produce large (1/2 to 1 inch in diameter) grapes that ripen around the second week of September. The way I usually find the ripe fruit is while walking or bicycling, a strong grape smell will grab my attention. I then follow my nose to where the clusters of ripe grapes are hanging on the vine. If you find enough grapes to pick and take home, you can make an excellent juice or purée for sorbets and other desserts. Just simmer the grapes in some water until they are soft, mash the pulp with a potato masher, then run though a food mill or sieve to extract the juice; leave the seeds behind. By the way, this wild grape juice or purée contains the same healthful resveratrol chemical that's in Japanese Knotweed (see Chapter Two). In contrast, Riverside Grapes are smaller than Fox/Summer Grapes (only about 1/4 to 1/2 inch in diameter) and tend to ripen a few weeks later; they have a tart, musky flavor that, although not very desirable in a raw fruit, makes a very distinctive and tasty jelly. Riverside Grape leaves, however, are more tender than Fox/Summer Grape leaves and so are better for use in stuffed grape leaves recipes. The undersides of Riverside Grape leaves are smooth and green, while those of the Fox/Summer Grape are finely woolly. The leaves (which also contain resveratrol) are best for harvesting during the last few weeks of spring, when they are large but still newly-formed. Simply blanch the leaves by dropping them into boiling water for about 20 seconds, then wrap each leaf around a spoonful of filling, and bake for around 45 minutes.

WILD LETTUCE (*Lactuca canadensis*) Wild Lettuces, the non-cultivated cousins of domesticated Lettuce, are closely related plants in the genus *Lactuca* (which means "milky" in Latin). All wild and cultivated Lettuces exude a whitish latex from cuts to the leaves or stalk. Wild Lettuces are commonly found along woods roads and edges and other sunny openings in the forest. Wild Lettuces tend to be more strongly flavored (i.e., bitter) than their cultivated counterparts, so generally are not worth eating raw, although one can still boil the young leaves (which strongly resemble oversized Dandelion leaves) for a minute or two and eat them as a cooked vegetable. There is, however, one species of Wild Lettuce which can be just about as tasty raw as any leaf lettuce you'd buy or grow: the annual Yellow Wild Lettuce (*Lactuca canadensis*), named for its small, Dandelion-like flowers. This species is distinguishable from other wild lettuces in that its blue-green leaves and stems are soft and smooth, and (most importantly) the terminal lobe on each leaf is long and skinny like a finger, whereas the terminal lobes of the other wild lettuces are broader and usually hairy. The plants can be harvested in Essex County from mid-May into early June (Limit yourself to picking a few leaves from each plant, or just the top cluster of leaves, in order to sustain the plant's ability to propagate). The leaves and stalk remain mild and tender even after the plants begin to "bolt" (produce a tall flower stalk). Eventually, though, the warmer weather will make *Lactuca canadensis* too tough and bitter to be worth eating.

 **WINTERCRESS** (*Barbarea vulgaris*) Wintercress, a member of the Brassicaceae or Mustard Family, is an extremely common farm and garden weed. The two edible portions of Wintercress are the leaves in the rosette stage, and the flower bud clusters in the "wild broccoli" stage (i.e. before the flowers open). The plant typically winters-over as rosettes (a prostrate whorl of leaves), which enable the plants to form 2-3 foot flower stalks and bloom the second week of May. Both of these plant parts need to be boiled a few minutes to reduce their pungency, after which they taste just like their close cultivated cousin, Broccoli Rabe. Wintercress, like most other members of the Mustard Family, are so loaded with vitamins, minerals and antioxidants that there are plenty left over even after the cooking process.

I have truly enjoyed sharing some of my knowledge of and fondness for the wonderful wild botanical treats we're blessed with in this region. I hope that the book enhances your appreciation and enjoyment of nature and the outdoors through responsibly partaking of its wild edible bounty. I wish you the best of luck in your future foraging endeavors, whether in Essex County, or wherever you happen to be. Please feel free to share with me your own stories about foraging successes and failures, favorite recipes, photographs, etc. You can contact me via e-mail (see copyright page) or perhaps I'll see you on one of my scheduled edible wild plant walks in Massachusetts and elsewhere in New England. In any case, Bon appetit!

Here are the results of a very good day of foraging: October 12, 2002. Going clockwise from the lower right corner of the photo, here's what I gathered that day: wild pears; King Bolete (Porcini) mushrooms (Boletus edulis), Horse mushrooms (Agaricus arvensis); Shagbark Hickory nuts; Autumn Olive berries; and more King Bolete and Horse mushrooms. (You are probably wondering what the barbecue grill is doing in the photo; I foraged for that, too: someone had put it out with their trash along the side of the road. I needed a grill at home, so I added it to the pile of stuff I gathered that day.)

BIBLIOGRAPHY:

A question that has come up frequently in my wild foods classes over the years is "What books would you recommend on this subject"? I have over 200 books in my library about foraging. Rather than just simply listing my favorites, I thought it would be more useful to provide capsule reviews of them as well as reviews of foraging books specifically aimed at a New England audience.

The book I most frequently recommend to people who don't yet have any good books on edible wild plants is Lee Allen Peterson's *A Field Guide to Edible Wild Plants of Eastern/Central North America* (Boston: Houghton Mifflin Co. ©1977; 330pp.; paperback with 75 color photographs; a revised edition was published in 1985 by Easton Press, Norwalk, CT). The plants are presented in a commonly-used field guide format, with categorizations such as flower color, size and/or branching habit. It is quite comprehensive, and I have only found about a half dozen mistakes, one of the biggest being a mistake of omission in that the author flatly refuses to explain to which botanical family each edible wild plant belongs.

Among my most well-used foraging books is *Wild Food*, by Roger Phillips (Boston: Little, Brown and Co. ©1986; 192pp.; paperback (folio-size)). This well-written and scrumptiously photographed book contains at least one tasty recipe for each species of plant and mushroom covered. In addition to taking excellent photos of the plants/mushrooms themselves in their natural habitats, Mr. Phillips also shot photos of the prepared dishes alongside their wild ingredients. If this book can't get your foraging juices flowing, nothing will. Though *Wild Food* is unfortunately out of print, used copies are readily available on the Web, and a British version is still in print and worth getting if you can't find the American version.

One book I am happy to say is back in print is Merritt Lyndon Fernald and Alfred Charles Kinsey's *Edible Wild Plants of Eastern North America* (New York: Harper and Row ©1943,1958; 452pp.; hardcover; republished by Dover Publications in 1996). This comprehensive book is still considered to be one of the foremost works on this subject, and served as one of my foraging "bibles" while first learning about edible wild plants in the 1970s. The plants are presented in botanical order (i.e., similar plant families are grouped together). The book also includes an extensive Bibliography containing references to a number of books from the 1800s and earlier.

Two excellent publications on wild edibles were produced by Essex County women during the "back to the land" movement of the 1960s and 1970s. The first is entitled, *Eating Wild: A Collection of Recipes Prepared, Tasted and Enjoyed by the Edible Wild Foods Committee of the Ipswich River Wildlife Sanctuary* (Topsfield, MA: Massachusetts Audubon Society, 1971; 114pp.; softcover). First published in 1971 and reprinted in 1974, *Eating Wild* includes recipes for nine of the plant species featured in this book, including Japanese Knotweed, Pokeweed, Milkweed, Sumac, Jerusalem Artichoke, Barberry, Black Locust, Sassafras and Cattail along with some other great wild edibles like Day Lily, Purslane, Dandelion and several wild mushrooms. This recipe book also contains brief descriptions and illustrations of many edible wild plants. Copies of *Eating Wild* should be available for sale at Massachusetts Audubon

Society's Ipswich River Wildlife Sanctuary's gift shop in Topsfield.

The second book is entitled *The Wild Gourmet: A Forager's Guide to the Finding and Cooking of Wild Foods* (Boston: David R. Godine ©1975; 160pp.; hardcover and softcover). *The Wild Gourmet* was written by Babette Brackett and MaryAnn Lash, two friends from Rockport, MA. In contrast to *Eating Wild*, which is a homespun, typed, spiral-bound affair, *The Wild Gourmet* is a beautifully printed, hardcover book with excellent illustrations. The book is arranged seasonally, with wild edible plant and mushroom descriptions and recipes presented throughout a calendar year as one is likely to find and eat them. Like *Eating Wild*, *The Wild Gourmet* includes recipes for more than half of the 14 plants featured in this book as well as many other plant and mushroom species available to foragers in Essex County.

Although any of Euell Gibbons' books are well worth reading, there are several I would like to recommend in particular. *Stalking the Wild Asparagus* (New York: David McKay Co. ©1962 (a 25th anniversary edition was published by A.C. Hood (dist. by Countryman Press, Woodstock, VT) in 1987); 303pp. hardcover and softcover) is the first and most well-known of Gibbons' books. The two dozen or so edible wild plants extensively discussed in the book are presented in chapters more or less in alphabetical order. The illustrations are sparse but serviceable, and the recipes are numerous and all tested by the author.

Stalking the Blue-eyed Scallop (New York: David McKay Co. ©1964; 332pp.; paperback and hardcover) is organized in a similar format and focuses on edible shellfish and other fish on both coasts (a small section is devoted to edible seaweeds and other edible plants of the seashore). One of Gibbons' books you may not have heard of but is well worth tracking down is *Euell Gibbons' Handbook of Edible Wild Plants* (Virginia Beach, VA: Donning (a Unilaw Library Book) ©1979; 319pp. hardcover). Gibbons died in 1975 while this work was underway, and co-author Gordon Tucker was recruited to complete the book while in college and graduate school. In contrast to Gibbons' earlier books, this one is quite comprehensive, as it provides short chapters on more than 100 edible wild plants found in North America.

Here are a few other books worth mentioning. *Identifying and Harvesting Edible and Medicinal Plants in Wild (and not so wild) Places* (New York: Hearst Books ©1994; 317pp.; softcover (folio-size)), by New York City-based foraging guru "Wildman" Steve Brill and Evelyn Dean, is very comprehensive, with the plants organized chronologically by habitat. The book also includes good black and white drawings of each plant, and many good recipes.

My Wild Friends: Free Food From Field and Forest (Northampton, MA: White Star Press ©1997; 264pp.; softcover (spiral-bound)), by Blanche Cybele Derby, contains over 40 "chapters," each focusing on a particular plant (or mushroom), and including personal anecdotes and recipes. Derby, a high school art teacher, drew marvelous and somewhat fanciful illustrations for the book. (Derby has since put out a second book, entitled, *More My Wild Friends*, which covers about two dozen more wild edibles.)

Another good book is *The Wild Food Gourmet: Fresh and savory food from nature* (Buffalo, NY: Firefly Books ©1998 (originally published in French in 1994 by Les Editions de l'Homme as La Cuisine des Champs) 174pp.; softcover). Author Anne Gardon grew up in Provénce (France) and now lives south of Montreal, and the 40 or so plant and mushroom species covered in the book can be found in the latter region. *The Wild Food Gourmet* contains dozens of recipes utilizing these plants/mushrooms, ranging from simple to complex preparations. It also features numerous gorgeous close-up color photos of wild plants and mushrooms and the gourmet dishes prepared from them.

My favorite wild foods cookbook is Cathy Johnson's *The Wild Foods Cookbook: Vegetables, salads, desserts, preserves and beverages from the field to your table* (New York: Stephen Greene Press/Pelham Books (Penguin) ©1989; 236pp.; softcover). The extensive and excellent recipes are sorted by type (salads, soups, main dishes, breads, preserves, desserts, beverages); main course dishes include fish and game recipes. A handful of well-known edible mushroom species are included as well as many helpful black and white illustrations.

Another favorite cookbook is Marilyn Kluger's *The Wild Flavor: Delectable wild foods to be found in field and forest and cooked in country kitchens* (Los Angeles: Jeremy P. Tarcher (distributed by Houghton Mifflin) ©1973; 285pp.; paperback) Although the book covers plants only (no wild meats), the recipes are well-organized by season and accompanied by stories of family foraging expeditions.

A recent (and highly valued) addition to my wild foods library is Sam Thayer's book *A Forager's Harvest: A Guide to Identifying, Harvesting and Preparing Edible Wild Plants* (Ogema, WI: Forager's Harvest © 2006; 360pp.; softcover). Sam hails from northern Wisconsin and his book provides extremely detailed information on 32 species of edible wild plants of that region (over half of which also grow in Essex County). The book is chock-full of practical advice on successful foraging techniques based on Sam's many years of direct personal experience. Numerous, high-quality color photographs illustrate the exact stage of each species for harvesting as well as poisonous look-alikes and their distinguishing features. The only minor drawbacks to the book are its limited geographic scale (many yummy species that don't grow so far north are left out) and its lack of recipes. Go to www.foragersharvest.com to order the book and for related info.

The book I most frequently recommend to aspiring mushroom hunters is Gary Lincoff's *The Audubon Society Field Guide to North American Mushrooms* (New York: Alfred A. Knopf ©1981; 926pp.; softcover). Although it is over two decades old, it remains a favorite among mushroom hunters. One drawback is that the book's photographs are labeled only by common (English) name, considered an unforgivable sin by serious mushroomers. Notwithstanding this fault, the coverage is comprehensive and the sketches and narrative descriptions are detailed and accurate. The book also includes an *in situ* photo of each mushroom that I have found to be particularly helpful in identifying and learning new species.

Although it focuses on Western mushrooms, David Arora's *All that the Rain Promises, and More... A Hip Pocket Guide to Western Mushrooms* (Berkeley, CA: Ten

Speed Press ©1991; 264pp.; softcover) includes many species found in New England. This book is very entertaining reading, with great anecdotes and color photos of mushrooms and people enjoying them.

Edible Wild Mushrooms of North America: A field to kitchen guide, Austin, TX: University of Texas Press ©1992; 254pp.; softcover), by David W. Fischer and Alan E. Bessette, provides good verbal descriptions and color photos of the tastiest wild mushroom species found in the Northeast, along with mouth-watering recipes and entertaining anecdotes.

I will end with two books specifically aimed at a New England foraging audience. *Wild Edible Plants of New England* (Yarmouth, ME: DeLorme Publishing Co. (republished by the Globe Pequot Press) ©1981; 217pp.; softcover), by Joan Richardson, is a fairly comprehensive work. Species are grouped by habitat, and edible and poisonous species discussed together, each marked with a "yum" or "yuck" symbol as appropriate. The book has 179 color photos, generally grouped by habitat, with similar-looking edible and (identified as such) poisonous species often presented on the same page. It also includes a short chapter on edible and poisonous mushrooms.

Foraging New England: Finding, Identifying and Preparing Edible Wild Foods and Medicinal Plants from Maine to Connecticut , by Tom Seymour (Guilford, CT: Globe Pequot Press (part of the Falcon Guide series) ©2002; 183pp.; paperback with 87 color photos) has plants grouped by habitat, and includes a handful of well-known and easy-to-recognize mushroom species. Although the book claims to cover New England, many well-known wild edibles found in southern New England such as Sassafras, Shagbark Hickory, Beach Plum, Mulberry and Pokeweed are left out. (The author hails from mid-coast Maine, and may have limited experience with edible species that don't grow that far north.) The book does include a well-written section on edible wild animals (bullfrogs and a half dozen shellfish species). Unfortunately, the book's color photos are of uneven quality (many are out of focus).

INDEX

NOTES

NOTES

New England Edible Wild Plants Checklist and Rarity Ranking.

Explanation of Rarity Ranking for Edible Wild Plants of New England Checklist:

I have given each edible wild plant listed a rarity ranking from A+ to C-; the higher the "grade," the less one needs to worry about any adverse ecological impacts from harvesting. A more detailed description of the grades follows.

A+   Plants that are exceedingly common throughout the Northeast U. S. and probably elsewhere; mostly introduced weeds and other invasive species. Most if not all plants with this rank are held in low regard by ecologists, as they tend to usurp habitat that would otherwise be occupied by less aggressive native species. Picking plants with this rank is unlikely to make a dent in their ability to perpetuate themselves at the harvesting spot or similar habitat nearby (not that the ecologists would mind, of course). Examples include Dandelions, Lambs Quarters and Chicory.

A   Very common plants, mostly introduced weeds but including some very common native species such as Cattail. These plants are not as ubiquitous or aggressive as the A+ rank, but they are common and numerous enough so that harvesting from all but the smallest patches will have no impact on the plant's availability for future harvests or affect its ecological niche. Examples include Day Lily, Evening Primrose and Dame's Rocket.

A-   Common plants, mostly introduced species that may be found in smaller patches here and there throughout the region and elsewhere. These plants are numerous enough as a whole so that one will run into them eventually even if none can be found within the immediate vicinity. Although plants in this category continue to have minor ecological value, a bit of care should be taken to ensure that enough plants are left while harvesting so that the plant may continue to exist at that location for the benefit of future foragers. Examples include Black Raspberries, Asiatic Dayflower and Catnip.

B+   Very common, mostly native species, most of which are found in good-sized patches. These plants do tend to be native or naturalized species that belong to the places where they are found, and thus often are relied upon by native fauna for food or otherwise. Nevertheless, these plants are usually numerous enough to be harvested for as much as one needs, and there should be plenty left over for humans and other animals. Examples include Blueberries, Crabapples and Sweet Fern.

B   This grade is for (mostly) native species that are locally abundant (i.e., they don't grow everywhere but when you do find them, you usually find more than a few of them), plus introduced species (Horseradish, e.g.) that are relatively uncommon. As these species tend to be somewhat particular about the type of habitat they will grow in, leave plenty at that location so they may continue to thrive there. Examples include Silverweed, Groundnut and Live-forever.

J
A+ Japanese Knotweed
B+ Jerusalem Artichoke
B+ Jewelweed
B+ Juneberry/Shadbush

K
B Kelp

L
C Labrador Tea
A+ Lambs Quarters
B Laver (Nori)
A- Linden (Basswood)
B Live-forever
C- Lotus, American
B Lunaria (Money Plant)

M
A Mallow, Common
B+ Maple
C Marsh Marigold
C+ May Apple
B- Mazzard Cherry
C Meadow Beauty
A Milkweed, Common
B Moosewood
B+ Mountain Ash
C Mountain Cranberry
A+ Mulberry

N
B Nannyberry
A Nettle, Stinging
C New Jersey Tea

O
B Orach
B- Ostrich Fern
A+ Ox-eye Daisy

P
B+ Partridgeberry
A Penny Cress
A+ Peppergrass
B+ Pickerelweed
A Pineapple Weed
A+ Plantain
B+ Pokeweed
A Poor Man's Pepper
C Prickly Pear
A+ Purslane

R
B+ Raspberry, Red
C Redbud
B+ Riverside Grape
A Rockweed

S
B- Salsify
B+ Sassafras
C Saxifrage
C Scotch Lovage
B- Sea Blite
B Sea Lettuce
B+ Sea Rocket
C Seacoast Angelica
B+ Shagbark Hickory
A+ Sheep Sorrel
A+ Shepherds Purse
B Silverweed
B- Slippery Elm
C Solomons Seal
A Sow Thistle
B+ Spatterdock
B+ Spicebush
C Spring Beauty
B- Spruce Gum
C Strawberry Blite
A+ Sumac
C Sweet Cicely
B+ Sweet Fern
B- Sweet Goldenrod

T
A+ Thistle, Bull
B- Toothwort
C Trailing Arbutus
C- Trillium
C- Trout Lily
C Twisted Stalk

V
A Violets, Common

W
C Waterberry
A Watercress
B+ White Oak
B White Water Lily
B Wild Apple
B- Wild Asparagus
B Wild Caraway
A+ Wild Carrot
A+ Wild Garlic
C+ Wild Ginger
C+ Wild Leek (Ramps)
A Wild Lettuce
B+ Wild Mint
A+ Wild Mustard
A+ Wild Onion
A Wild Parsnip
B- Wild Raisin
B- Wild Rice
A Wild Rose
B+ Wild Strawberry
A Wild Thyme
B Wineberry
A+ Wintercress
B+ Wintergreen
A+ Wood Sorrel
B+ Wood Nettle

Y
B+ Yellow Birch
B- Yucca

New England Edible Wild Plants Checklist and Rarity Ranking.

NOTE: The letter "grade" before each plant name indicates its relative rarity in New England; the "lower" the grade, the greater care must be used in harvesting it. See notes on reverse side for a more detailed explanation.

A
A+ Amaranth
B- Arrowhead
A+ Autumn Olive
B Azalea galls

B
A- Barberry, European
B Bayberry
B Beach Pea
C+ Beach Plum
A+ Bedstraw, Common
B+ Beech
C+ Bellwort
B+ Black Birch
A Black Cherry
A+ Black Locust
A- Black Nightshade
A- Black Raspberry
B Black Walnut
B+ Blackberry
A- Bladder Campion
B+ Blueberry
A Bracken Fern
C Bugleweed
C Bulrush, Common
B+ Bunchberry
A+ Burdock
B Butternut

C
B- Calamus (Sweet Flag)
A+ Canada Mayflower
C Carrion Flower
A Cat Brier

A- Catnip
A Cattail
A- Charlock
C Chestnut
B+ Chestnut Oak
A+ Chickweed
A+ Chicory
B+ Choke Cherry
A Chufa
B+ Cinquefoil
A Cleavers
B+ Clintonia (Corn Lily)
A Clover
A Coltsfoot
B Cow Parsnip
B+ Crabapple
B Cranberry, Bog
C- Creeping Snowberry
C Cuckoo Flower
A+ Curled Dock

D
A Dame's Rocket
B Dangleberry
A+ Dandelion
A Day Lily
A- Dayflower, Asiatic
B+ Dewberry
B Dulse
C Dwarf Ginseng

E
B+ Elderberry, Black
A Evening Primrose

F
C+ False Solomons Seal
B Fire Cherry
B Fireweed
B Flowering Raspberry
B+ Fox Grape
A Foxtail Grass

G
A+ Galinsoga
A+ Garlic Mustard
A Giant Knotweed
B Gingko
B+ Glasswort
B Gooseberries/Currants
B Goosetongue
B Ground Cherry
B Groundnut

H
B+ Hackberry
B+ Hawthorn
B Hazelnut
B- Highbush Cranberry
B Hog Peanut
B Hops
B Horseradish
B+ Huckleberry

I
C+ Indian Cucumber
B+ Irish Moss

B- Plants in this category tend to be somewhat elusive, tending only to appear in a small portion of the habitat that is otherwise suitable for them. Occasionally, they can be found in large patches, but even then one must take extra care to harvest carefully and judiciously so as not to endanger the plant's continued ability to thrive at that location. Examples include Ostrich Fern, Toothwort and Wild Rice.

C+ Grade C plants are those that are either rare enough that careless harvesting could easily harm them and/or the wild creatures that depend on them; or are considered to have other values beyond edibility (e.g. aesthetic) so that one should think twice before picking them. C+ plants are the most numerous of the group and can be safely and plentifully harvested only if one of every dozen or so plants present are taken, or (for parts harvested other than the whole plant or root) if the plant is left intact as much as possible to ensure its continued healthy existence. C+ plants include Indian Cucumber, May Apple and Wild Leek.

C Plants with this grade tend to be either confined to very specialized habitats that are rare in the region, or are more common but are considered by many as too pretty to pick. Nevertheless, it is OK to pick them as long as one is very careful that the picking makes a negligible impact in the patch's health or appearance. Examples include Carrion Flower, Marsh Marigold and Spring Beauty.

C- This "lowest" grade is for some native wildflowers and/or species that, due to their rarity, are on the rare species list for at least one New England state. They should not be picked in any state where they are on that state's rare species list. Nevertheless, they can be sparingly harvested in the places in New England where they are relatively abundant. Examples include Creeping Snowberry and Mountain Cranberry, both extremely rare in Southern New England but abundant enough to harvest at some locations at higher elevations and/or latitudes.

Last but not least, it is important to note that the portion of the plant one is harvesting often has a great bearing on whether the picking is innocuous or potentially harmful. Digging plants up to harvest the edible roots is usually more traumatic than merely picking berries, but some plants don't mind (and may actually benefit) from some thinning below the ground (Day Lilies, Jerusalem Artichokes, etc.). So the rules for responsible foraging go beyond rarity considerations to the impact of harvesting on various plant parts, aesthetic value, wildlife food value, rare look-alikes and other concerns. It is better in the long run to learn each plant's individual situation rather than unduly relying upon its letter ranking in this checklist.

Plant (part) in season:	Blueberries	May Apples	Black Cherries	Elderberry berries	Sumac berries	Ground Cherries	Hazelnuts	Beach Plums	Fox Grapes	Acorns from "soft" Oak species	Riverside Grapes	Cranberries	Hickory Nuts	Crabapples	Chestnuts	Black Walnuts
Dec.–Mar.																
Nov. 24–30																
Nov. 16–23																
Nov. 9–15																
Nov. 1–8						▓					▓					
Oct. 24–31					▓		·				▓	▓	▓			▓
Oct. 16–23					▓					▓	▓	▓	▓	▓	▓	▓
Oct. 9–15										▓	▓	▓	▓	▓	▓	
Oct. 1–8										▓	▓		▓	▓		
Sep. 24–30			▓	▓	▓			▓			▓			▓		
Sep. 16–23			▓	▓	▓			▓	▓					▓		
Sep. 9–15			▓	▓	▓	▓		▓	▓							
Sep. 1–8			▓	▓		▓		▓								
Aug. 24–31			▓	▓	▓	▓										
Aug. 16–23			▓			▓										
Aug. 9–15	▓	▓														
Aug. 1–8	▓	▓														
July 24–31	▓															
July 16–23	▓															
July 9–15																
July 1–8																
June 24–30																
June 16–23																
June 9–15																
June 1–8																
May 24–31																
May 16–23																
May 9–15																
May 1–8																
Apr. 24–30																
Apr. 16–23																
Apr. 9–15																
Apr. 1–8																
Dec./Mar.																

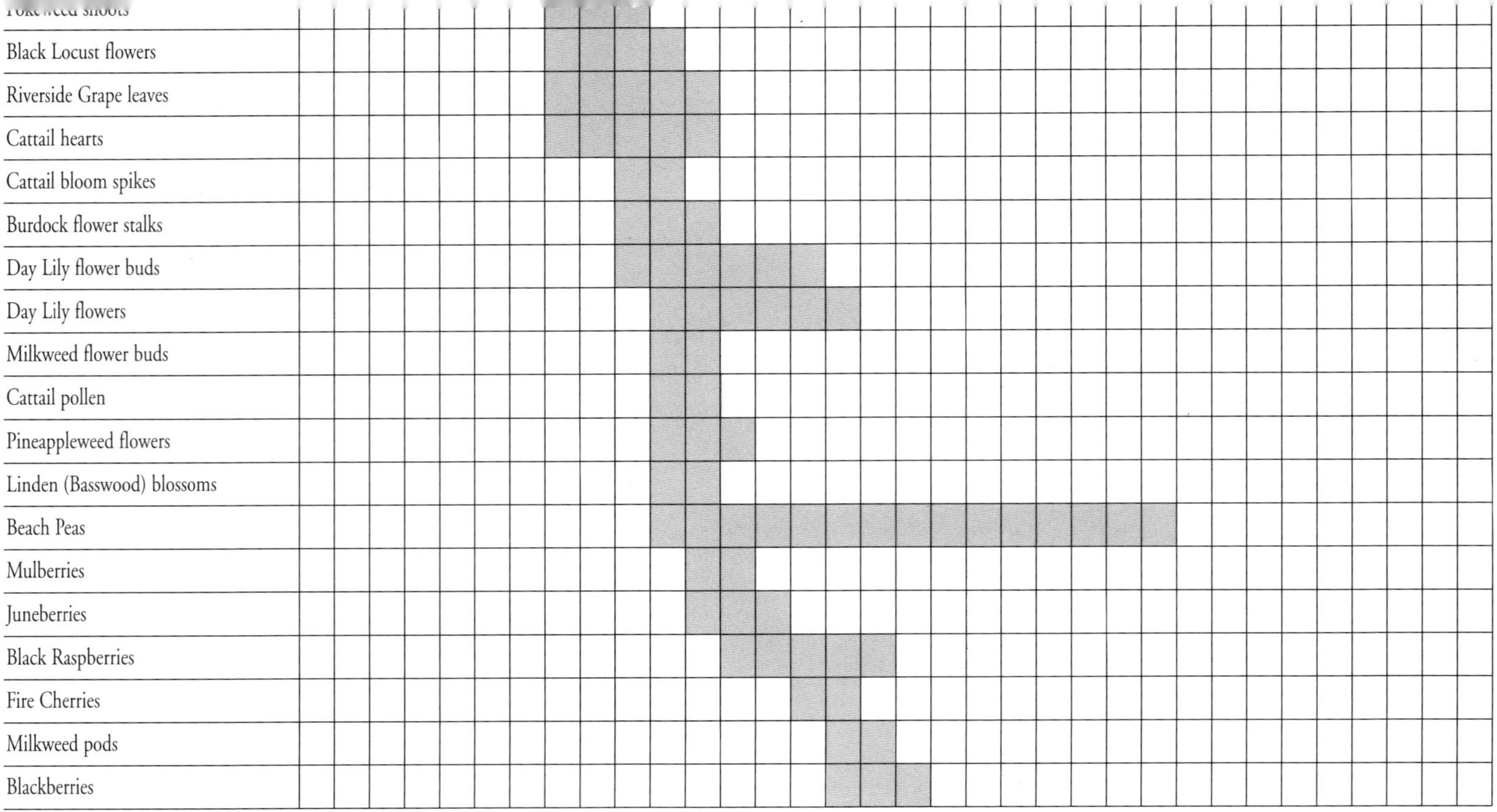

Black Locust flowers

Riverside Grape leaves

Cattail hearts

Cattail bloom spikes

Burdock flower stalks

Day Lily flower buds

Day Lily flowers

Milkweed flower buds

Cattail pollen

Pineappleweed flowers

Linden (Basswood) blossoms

Beach Peas

Mulberries

Juneberries

Black Raspberries

Fire Cherries

Milkweed pods

Blackberries

When to Pick Edible Plants in New England. (in chronological order)

Prepared by Russ Cohen - Third Edition - July 2014.

Plant (part) in season:	Dec./Mar.	Apr. 1-8	Apr. 9-15	Apr. 16-23	Apr. 24-30	May 1-8	May 9-15	May 16-23	May 24-31	June 1-8	June 9-15	June 16-23	June 24-30	July 1-8	July 9-15	July 16-23	July 24-31	Aug. 1-8	Aug. 9-15	Aug. 16-23	Aug.24-31	Sep. 1-8	Sep. 9-15	Sep. 16-23	Sep.24-30	Oct. 1-8	Oct. 9-15	Oct. 16-23	Oct. 24-31	Nov. 1-8	Nov. 9-15	Nov. 16-23	Nov.24-30	Dec.-Mar.
Stinging Nettle greens		■	■	■	■																													
Ostrich Fern fiddleheads			■	■	■																													
Marsh Marigold leaves				■	■																													
Violet flowers + leaves					■	■																												
Japanese Knotweed shoots						■	■																											
Dandelion flower buds						■	■																											
Salsify greens						■																												
Garlic Mustard stems/buds/flowers						■	■																											
Japanese Knotweed stalks						■	■																											
Wintercress flower buds						■																												
Dame's Rocket flowers									■	■	■																							
Milkweed shoots								■	■																									
Ox-eye Daisy leaves + flower buds							■	■	■																									
Elderberry flowers									■	■																								
Carrion Flower shoots								■	■	■																								
Wild Lettuce								■	■	■																								

| Autumn Olive berries |
| Barberry berries |
| Evening Primrose roots |
| Burdock roots |
| Wild Carrots |
| Maple sap |
| Arrowhead tubers |

Notes:

(1) These dates are for the Greater Boston region. In some cases, you may be able to "turn the clock back" and extend the season of availability for some plant parts by moving north and/or higher in elevation (the growing season is typically about a week behind for every 50 miles you move north).

(2) The plants/plant parts listed in this table include only those items that: a) are known to occur in the Greater Boston area; b) are at the tastier end of the wild edibles spectrum; and c) have a limited and relatively definable season of availability. Although certainly tasty and worth gathering, Sassafras roots and Groundnut tubers are not included, for example, because they are available year-round. Other plants, like Chickweed and Wood Sorrel, are not included because their availability depends at least as much on recent weather patterns (moisture and temperature) as on the time of year. Future editions of this table will include more plants/plant parts as my data set expands each year.

(3) This table lists plants by their common names. Many plants have

Husk Tomato or Strawberry Tomato. I simply chose the common name I am most familiar with. So if you don't see a particular plant you know to be edible and abundant in the Greater Boston area, it may be listed under another common name. In addition, one name may represent two or more species; "Maple," for example, includes all the local native Maple species such as Sugar Maple, Red Maple and Box Elder, all of which may be tapped for sap which can be boiled down to make maple syrup and sugar.

(4) WARNING: Just because a plant/plant part is listed, do not assume it is tasty or even safe to eat in its raw state. Many plants, such as Milkweed and Marsh Marigold, must be boiled before eating to reduce their bitter and/or toxic content to a safe and palatable level. Other plants on the list, such as Black Locust and Black Cherry, have poisonous as well as edible parts. Please consult a competent guide on edible wild plants if you are unsure about identification, preparation methods or other important details.

More info on Russ Cohen's Wild Food walks/courses: eatwild@rcn.com or http://users.rcn.com/eatwild/sched.htm.

Plant (part) in season:	Dec./Mar.	Apr. 1-8	Apr. 9-15	Apr. 16-23	Apr. 24-30	May 1-8	May 9-15	May 16-23	May 24-31	June 1-8	June 9-15	June 16-23	June 24-30	July 1-8	July 9-15	July 16-23	July 24-31	Aug. 1-8	Aug. 9-15	Aug. 16-23	Aug. 24-31	Sep. 1-8	Sep. 9-15	Sep. 16-23	Sep. 24-30	Oct. 1-8	Oct. 9-15	Oct. 16-23	Oct. 24-31	Nov. 1-8	Nov. 9-15	Nov. 16-23	Nov. 24-30	Dec.-Mar.
Japanese Knotweed stalks					▓	▓	▓																											
Juneberries												▓	▓	▓																				
Linden (Basswood) blossoms											▓	▓																						
Maple sap	▓																																	▓
Marsh Marigold leaves				▓	▓																													
May Apples																		▓	▓															
Milkweed flower buds																▓	▓																	
Milkweed pods											▓	▓																						
Milkweed shoots								▓																										
Mulberries													▓																					
Ostrich Fern Fiddleheads																																		
Ox-eye Daisy leaves + flower buds				▓					▓																									
Pineappleweed flowers													▓																					
Pokeweed shoots									▓	▓																								
Riverside Grape leaves							▓	▓	▓	▓		▓											▓	▓										
Riverside Grapes																												▓	▓	▓				

Cattail pollen

Chestnuts

Crabapples

Cranberries

Dame's Rocket flowers

Dandelion flower buds

Day Lily flower buds

Day Lily flowers

Elderberry berries

Elderberry flowers

Evening Primrose roots

Fire Cherries

Fox Grapes

Garlic Mustard stems/buds/flowers

Ground Cherries

Hazelnuts

Hickory Nuts

Japanese Knotweed shoots

When to Pick Wild Edible Plants in New England. (in alphabetical order)

Prepared by Russ Cohen - Third Edition – July 2014

Plant (part) in season:	Dec./Mar.	Apr. 1-8	Apr. 9-15	Apr. 16-23	Apr. 24-30	May 1-8	May 9-15	May 16-23	May 24-31	June 1-8	June 9-15	June 16-23	June 24-30	July 1-8	July 9-15	July 16-23	July 24-31	Aug. 1-8	Aug. 9-15	Aug. 16-23	Aug. 24-31	Sep. 1-8	Sep. 9-15	Sep. 16-23	Sep. 24-30	Oct. 1-8	Oct. 9-15	Oct. 16-23	Oct. 24-31	Nov. 1-8	Nov. 9-15	Nov. 16-23	Nov. 24-30	Dec.-Mar.
Acorns from "soft" Oak species																									X	X								
Arrowhead tubers	X																																	X
Autumn Olive berries																											X	X	X	X	X	X	X	X
Barberry berries	X	X																									X	X	X	X	X	X	X	X
Beach Peas																		X	X	X	X	X	X	X	X									
Beach Plums																							X	X	X									
Black Cherries																								X	X									
Black Locust flowers								X	X	X	X																							
Black Raspberries													X	X	X	X	X																	
Black Walnuts																										X	X	X	X					
Blackberries																	X	X	X															
Blueberries															X	X	X	X	X															
Burdock flower stalks										X	X	X																						
Burdock roots	X		X																											X	X		X	X
Carrion Flower shoots								X	X	X	X																							
Cattail bloom spikes											X	X																						

| Salsify greens |
| Stinging Nettle greens |
| Sumac berries |
| Violet flowers + leaves |
| Wild Carrots |
| Wild Lettuce |
| Wintercress flower buds |

Notes:

(1) These dates are for the Greater Boston region. In some cases, you may be able to "turn the clock back" and extend the season of availability for some plant parts by moving north and/or higher in elevation (the growing season is typically about a week behind for every 50 miles you move north).

(2) The plants/plant parts listed in this table include only those items that: a) are known to occur in the Greater Boston area; b) are at the tastier end of the wild edibles spectrum; and c) have a limited and relatively definable season of availability. Although certainly tasty and worth gathering, Sassafras roots and Groundnut tubers are not included, for example, because they are available year-round. Other plants, like Chickweed and Wood Sorrel, are not included because their availability depends at least as much on recent weather patterns (moisture and temperature) as on the time of year. Future editions of this table will include more plants/plant parts as my data set expands each year.

(3) This table lists plants by their common names. Many plants have two or more common names, e.g., Ground Cherry is also called Husk Tomato or Strawberry Tomato. I simply chose the common name I am most familiar with. So if you don't see a particular plant you know to be edible and abundant in the Greater Boston area, it may be listed under another common name. In addition, one name may represent two or more species; "Maple," for example, includes all the local native Maple species such as Sugar Maple, Red Maple and Box Elder, all of which may be tapped for sap which can be boiled down to make maple syrup and sugar.

(4) WARNING: Just because a plant/plant part is listed, do not assume it is tasty or even safe to eat in its raw state. Many plants, such as Milkweed and Marsh Marigold, must be boiled before eating to reduce their bitter and/or toxic content to a safe and palatable level. Other plants on the list, such as Black Locust and Black Cherry, have poisonous as well as edible parts. Please consult a competent guide on edible wild plants if you are unsure about identification, preparation methods or other important details.

More info on Russ Cohen's Wild Food walks/courses: eatwild@rcn.com or http://users.rcn.com/eatwild/sched.htm.